'92

1ᴾᵀ
8/13/10

Back Roads of the Central Coast

Second Edition

by Ron Stob

Bear Flag Books   1998   Arroyo Grande CA

©1986, 1990, 1992 Ron Stob

All rights reserved under International and Pan-American Conventions. No part of this book may be reproduced, stored in a retrieval system, or transmitted in any form or by any means, electronic, mechanical, recording or otherwise, without express written permission of the author, except for education photocopying as provided by Public Law 94-533 (Secs. 106, 107 and 108, title 17, *United States Code.*), and for brief quotations in book reviews.

Library of Congress Cataloging-in-Publication Data

Stob, Ron, 1932–
    Back roads of the central coast.

    Includes index.
    1. California--Description and travel--1981-
--Guide-books.   2. Automobiles--Road guides--California.
I. Title.
F859.3.S82   1986   917.94'0453   86-10840
ISBN 0-939919-28-1

Printed in the United States of America

Published by Bear Flag Books/A Division of Padre Productions
            P.O. Box 840
            Arroyo Grande CA 93421-0840

Contents

Foreword

Those of us who live on the California Central Coast know deep in our hearts that we are among the most-blessed peoples of the world. This is God's Country, a land of beauty, marvelous climate and intense feeling. It is a land that combines most of nature's wonders in a relatively small area. It is a land of hidden splendors and enormous possibilities.

This is what Ron Stob writes about—the possibilities for reflection, peace of mind and renewal that exist within our reach.

All of us who live here—from the native to the recent arrival—often leave the territory of our own backyard unexplored.

Ron Stob, himself a transplant from Chicago, follows those little signposts as they beckon him on the back roads, and he takes us there with him on his adventures.

Now, in one volume, he presents the best of those "Back Roads" tales. In them, I would hope that you will find inspiration to explore the wonders that lie so close to us in every direction. The good life is out there, within easy reach of San Luis Obispo, Cambria or Paso Robles. This book is your guide to help you find it.

George DeBord, Editor
San Luis Obispo *Telegram-Tribune*

iv

Introduction

It has been a pleasure working with Ron Stob, editing his bi-weekly contributions to our Saturday *Focus* magazine. His "Back Roads" columns —whether a narrative of his experiences hiking along seaside terraces, of horseback rides in the wilderness, or of motoring along country roads where almond trees bloom—are always an adventure to read. They make me want to go to these places.

"Back Roads" is a very special form of "entertainment" in the *Focus* arts and entertainment magazine. Ron's column, at its best, does what great literature, good films and fine art do: it both informs and inspires its audience.

So sit back and enjoy this, the best of "Back Roads."

Diane Holt, *Focus* Editor
San Luis Obispo *Telegram-Tribune*

Publisher's Note

Ron Stob's columns published in the *Telegram-Tribune* guide readers to delightful outings. Every effort has been made to bring the information up to date for this second edition of *Back Roads of the Central Coast*. However, it is advisable to call numbers listed in the chapters to confirm weather conditions, hours open to the public, prices and other factors subject to change.

We take this opportunity to thank our retailers and distributors and the readers who have contributed to the success of *Back Roads of the Central Coast* and the companion edition, *More Back Roads of the Central Coast*. Changes and suggestions are welcome; please mail to the Publisher, P.O. Box 840, Arroyo Grande CA 93421-0840.

Lachlan P. MacDonald Bear Flag Books

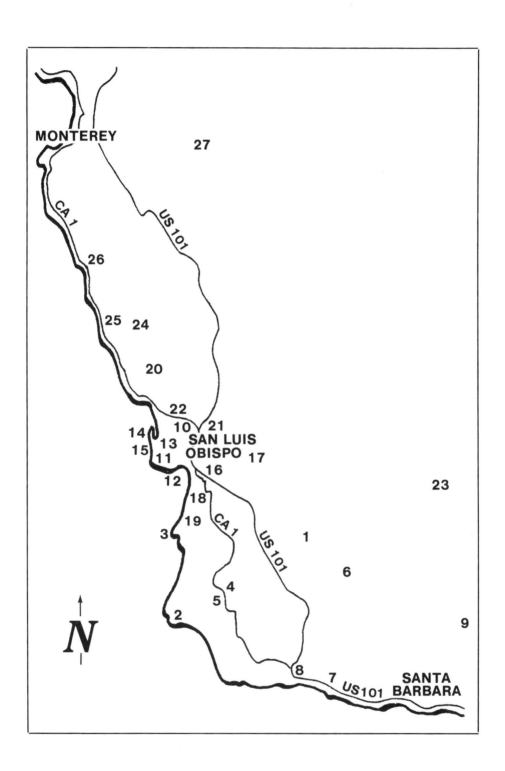

I Points South

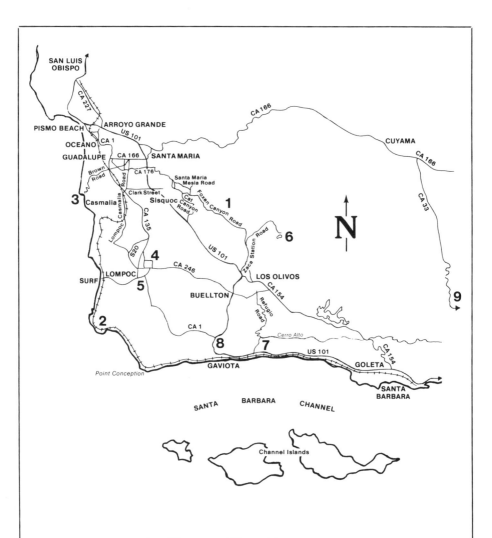

1 **Sisquoc River Valley**
2 **A Southbound Odyssey**
3 **Point Sal**
4 **La Purisima Mission**
5 **Lompoc Flower Festival**
6 **Zaca Lake**
7 **Circle Bar B**
8 **Gaviota Hot Springs**
9 **Sespe-Frazier Wilderness**

1—Sisquoc River Valley—
A Day of Vines and Wines Along
an Old Stage Coach Road

> Eat thy bread with joy, and drink thy wine with a
> merry heart . . . enjoy life with the woman you love
> all the days of your alloted span here under the sun.
> *Ecclesiastes 9*

Those words were not written in the Sisquoc River Valley, but they ring true here where towering mountains nurture a rich valley of vineyards, historic adobes and soul-refreshing beauty.

From Santa Maria we left Route 101 on Betteravia Road (Route 176) and headed east, setting the odometer to pinpoint the way. Route 176 heads eastward across flat fields of produce flourishing in the silty alluvia of the Santa Maria and Sisquoc Rivers.

After a few sharp 90-degree turns we came to Santa Maria Mesa Road and turned left. In 2.1 miles (9.6 from Route 101) we passed over the bridge on the Sisquoc and came by Coast Rock on the right. The second roadway on the left past the bridge is a paved, private road that goes to several ranches. About a mile down this road is the Juan Pacifico Adobe (1857) on the left side of the road.

The adobe is a white-stuccoed building with a six-foot overhanging porch that gives shade in the summer and protection from the winter rains. The first level is a large living room with fireplace, and bedrooms on either end. On the east end an encased stairway leads to the attic, which was used as a dormitory sleeping room for the working men.

Through the streaked bubble glass we imagined the life of this early California family situated around the big stone fireplace. The kitchen was outdoors and all the cooking and baking was done in beehive ovens in the yard.

9

The San Ramone Chapel in the Sisquoc River Valley.

We retraced our way along the Santa Maria Mesa Road back to Route 176, turned left and came into the town of Garey at 12.1 miles.

M. Garey came to these parts in 1890 to convert the land from dry land crops to orchards. Across from the flat front general store is a blacksmith shop.

On the way to the next town of Sisquoc we observed cattle grazing in lush valleys among oil pumpers, the clue to the beginning of this little burg. A block from town is the Blochman School with its collection of bells taken from outlying historical schools that were consolidated to form the present school.

More than 130 years ago a visting priest from the Santa Ynez Mission came to the Sisquoc Valley to marry young couples and baptize babies under the shade of the poplar trees behind the school.

Sisquoc began at the time of the Palmer-Stendell oil gusher (1910), which signaled a new beginning for this valley and the hills south. The Sisquoc store served as a general mercantile supply base for the burgeoning oil well community. The Pacific Coast Railroad ran a spur over from Santa Maria to Garey and Sisquoc and up Palmer Road. Oil and supplies went from there back to Santa Maria and over to the third pier at Avila, where the Pacific Coast Mail steamship Line transported people and goods up and down the coast.

Route 176 ends in Sisquoc and Cat Canyon Road proceeds straight ahead. We turned left on Foxen Canyon Road, a stage coach trail that was the principal route between Santa Maria and Santa Barbara from 1850–1920. This is my favorite way to travel to Santa Barbara when I have time. It's a serenely beautiful drive through barley fields, vineyards and alongside old stage coach stops. Bicycling this valley is very popular because of its scenic beauty and low traffic.

One and a half miles from Sisquoc, on Foxen Canyon Road, are the remains of the Ramone-Goodchild adobe. It's on the right side of the road, situated on a bench beyond a row of eucalyptus that were planted around 1870. Look for twin date palms on the south edge of the grounds.

At 17.2 miles we passed Byron Vineyards, and in the distance saw the twin spires of the San Ramone Chapel. At 18.0 we came to the chapel and the private road to the Rancho Sisquoc Winery. Because of vandalism, the chapel cemetery, in the rear that bears the remains of Benjamin Foxen, Juan Pacifico and others, is fenced and locked.

The chapel was built of redwood in 1875 by Romana Foxen (daughter of Benjamin) and her husband, Frederick Wickenden, with the help of neighboring families. The chapel shows the transition from adobe styles to frame. The interior is simple pine board with Gothic windows and a dozen pews. It's still in use by the families of early settlers who remain in the valley.

Two miles further on the road alongside the chapel is the Rancho Sisquoc Winery, an extraordinarily pleasant hideaway winery among country vernacular frame farm buildings and grassy lawns. The little brown winery lies tucked between the wisteria-garlanded cottages where oenologist Harold Pfeiffer serves his undistributed wines to a clientele looking for the obscure and unusual. A pleasant picnic area is behind the tasting room.

The Flood family of San Francisco owns 36,000 acres of this range-land and 200 acres of vineyards along the Sisquoc River.

We reset the odometer to zero when we got back out to the chapel on Foxen Canyon Road, and turned left.

At 1.8 miles from the chapel is an old stage coach stop, the Frederick Wickenden adobe, a large white frame house on the right side across from a red barn of the Rancho Tinaquaic. This sprawling wood home is built over a small adobe constructed by Ramona Foxen and Frederick Wickenden. Wooden porches and a second-story were later additions. The rutted ground where the stage coach horses made their turn-around can still be seen in the side yard on the right.

At 3.1 miles from the San Ramone Chapel we came to a memorial marker. It designates the spot where John C. Fremont camped in 1846 after being warned by Benjamin Foxen of an ambush at Gaviota Pass. Foxen's son guided Fremont through San Marcos Pass on Christmas Day, 1846. The next day Fremont made a surprise attack on Santa Barbara and took it for the U.S. Three weeks later, on January 13, 1847, Mexico ceded California to the U.S.

Down the road about a mile I saw two ranchers standing knee high in a barley field, near the site of Foxen's first adobe (1837), designated by a marker on a fence post hidden in the weeds. Foxen was burned out of his first adobe by Mexican Californians who considered him a traitor for helping John C. Fremont. The ranchers came over to the fence and we shot the breeze about times past... and the present, and the lack of rain. Broken clouds shot bursts of light across the green hills that loped toward the distant San Rafael Mountains.

"When I was young the country was old. Now I got old and the country is the same age yet. I look at those hills and they're just as new and pretty as when I was a kid," Louis Costa mused.

We stood there, silent, getting drunk on the beauty of the valley. The oats and barley waved in the wind, putting the hills in motion . . . while meadowlarks sang from the barbed wire fence.

The last winery in the Sisquoc Valley on Foxen Canyon Road is the Zaca Mesa Winery, at 9.2 miles from the chapel. Since 1976 it has grown to over 70,000 cases a year distributed nationally. They are very proud of their French-style Sirah and Pinot Noir. During the crush in the fall would be a particularly pleasant time to come here.

A mile beyond Zaca Mesa Winery is the road to Zaca Lake Resort. Turn left and travel seven miles on the rough country road to the lake and resort.

From the entrance to Zaca Lake the road winds over a ridge to the Santa Ynez Valley on the other side, where cattle stood belly deep in waving grass. At 12.2 miles the road to Zaca Lake takes a sharp 120-degree left turn through the Zaca Ranch gate. It's a seven mile drive up to the lake and restaurant there. (See Chapter 6.)

The road turns 90-degrees right past the Douglas Vineyards. At 14.2 Foxen Canyon Road (and the old stagecoach road) go left to Los Olivos, a few miles away. The stagecoach stopped at Mattei's Tavern on Route 154, and at Cold Springs Tavern, near the summit of San Marcos Pass, before it descended into Santa Barbara.

If you continue straight ahead on Zaca Station Road, you can wheel into the Firestone Winery at 14.8 miles. Brooks Firestone, a grandson in the Firestone Tire family, got tired of the corporate life and learned the nuts and bolts of making wine in the Santa Ynez Valley. Many consider his new efforts tireless.

Firestone has labeled most of his grape vines, a nice touch if you like to identify the grapes as they mature on the vine. The winery is open daily from 10–4, but closed on Sunday.

Whether you are simply out for a joy ride or looking for a scenic drive to Santa Barbara, consider Foxen Canyon Road . . .

> Come, my beloved,
> > let us go forth into the fields,
> > and lodge in the villages
> let us go out early to the vineyards
> > and see whether the vines have budded,
> whether the grape blossoms have opened
> > and the pomegranates are in bloom.
> There I will give you my love.
> > > > *Song of Solomon*, Ch. 7.

Amtrak passing through Price Canyon.

2—A Southbound Odyssey, by Rail Past Lighthouses and Pounding Surf

The voice of the station agent in San Luis Obispo was getting travelers ready for a southbound odyssey.

"Arriving in five minutes, train #11, the Coast Starlight, going south to Santa Barbara, Oxnard, Glendale, Los Angeles, Indio, Phoenix, El Paso, Houston and New Orleans; with connecting trains south to San Diego. Chair cars will be down to your left of the station entrance and sleeping cars will be right in front. Please be ready to board. Thank you for traveling Amtrak, and have a pleasant trip."

I was only going to Santa Barbara, but I was excited as the train pulled into the station. Hearing names of places like Indio, El Paso and New Orleans made me dream. It was a shopping list of interesting places, that set my mind loose on a fantasy trip.

The last time I was on a train was going through Illinois on the Illinois Central; must have been ten years ago: "Passin' towns that have no names, freight yards full of old black men, graveyards of rusted automobiles." What a difference.

The train rounded the corner, a huge grimy engine pulling a string of silver cars. Porters jumped out as the train came to a stop and a dribble of people stepped out into the San Luis Obispo sunshine to be embraced by waiting family and friends.

I was introduced to a service attendant who took me to the crew's quarters in a vintage car behind the engine. As the train began to move, the clicking of the rails brought back memories. Walking through the sleeper cars I met a kindly black porter with handsome graying hair, who showed me the finer side of life on Amtrak—miniature studios with tiny baths and showers, and beds that fold down in the night. Then through the coach car, which resembles an airplane or bus interior. A confusing

15

array of figures lounged and slept. The atmosphere suggested they all had been there for some time.

I moved on to the lounge car, an all-glass living room on wheels. This is where I wanted to be. I was amazed at how quiet and smooth the ride was. No swaying or pitching, not even the romantic clicking of the rails. Just gliding along on pneumatic suspension. These are the cars of the '80s: slick, comfortable and quiet as a Mercedes-Benz.

Sitting in a semicircular arrangement of lounge chairs I began to get my bearings. There are the vineyards of Edna, golden against the purple Santa Lucia Mountains. We crossed under Highway 227 near the airport and ran parallel to it before we entered Price Canyon. The train came to a stop along a siding while train #14 from Santa Barbara came through. This was a good time to go to the bar where soft drinks, wine and liquor are served.

People don't stay strangers on a train for very long. I met Flo Burger who had been on the train from Ithaca, N.Y., taking advantage of one of those Amtrak specials—anywhere in the U.S. in 45 days with three stop-overs, for $259 (1989).

She was the image of everybody's aunt from somewhere distant, sitting comfortably with a lapful of knitting, dividing her attention between conversation and the passing scenery. Bob Childs, a retired agricultural expert from back East asked questions about California crops and soils.

I asked Ken Nowak, a pilot in the Air Force Reserve, why he was traveling Amtrak. "You just can't see America from the air, and cars don't go where trains go. When you're driving you've got to concentrate on the road, but here you just relax and look out." He was right.

Train riders have a keen interest in the people and geography of America. They have seen the diversity of neighborhoods and country-side and some sit with maps and brochures following their course across the land.

The train was moving again; picking up speed. We cut under High-way 101 and I could see the Seaview Motel, then a pretty little marsh behind Hacienda Del Sol Trailer Court. Now we were along Route 1 by Pismo Beach State Park—and Oceano and the produce fields. There's the historic Coffee-Rice House across the fields of cabbage and brussel sprouts.

Running up on to the Nipomo Mesa we paralled Route 1 again. The back side of the Nipomo Dunes were visible and I found myself giving a guided tour to people from New York and Philadelphia and Cincinnati.

In Guadalupe there's a big switch yard and we inched by freight trains and box cars loaded with California produce bound for the East. Monopoly-size houses lined the rails, back yards full of cages with ducks and chickens. A little pink house with a large picture window looked out onto the tracks. A gaudy gold-laced banner wished train travelers a Merry Christmas. Humorous and touching. Through the neighborhood bungalows a Spanish church stood like a shepherd among sheep.

The train slid out of Guadalupe approaching Casmalia, running next to Route 1 for a while, then next to Black Road and Lompoc-Casmalia Road. Sunlight pierced through storms clouds and shimmered off the hills brushed with newborn grass.

There's a sharp turn in the tracks then as it goes past the town of Casmalia and heads straight toward the ocean. As we approached the headlands and dunes we turned left (south) again and I could see Point Sal to the right (north).

Rolling white surf crashed against the shore. It was one of those dramatic moments when mountains, sea, sky and sunlight come together in breathtaking beauty. Hills of ice plant, as red as tomatoes, ran to the sea.

I was astounded. I had hiked a lot of this coastline and have been down here with my car where roads are available, but I've never seen anything like this. Southern Pacific couldn't have built the rails any closer to the frothing surf. Sated train riders and new aboards alike were struck with the beauty. Everyone moved to the oceanside of the lounge car applauding the views along our coast. Mile after mile of picturesque coastline was on our right and Vandenberg Air Force Base towers and launch pads to our left.

Across the mouth of the Santa Ynez River we passed above Ocean Beach County Park, near Surf. Campers waved as we went by. We all waved back. Rimming the coast we sped through the U.S. Naval Missile Facility. At Point Arguello and Rocky Point I could see the white rectangular lighthouse and the homes and workshops of the lighthouse keepers. Automated devices installed in 1970 eliminated the need for personnel, but the buildings still stand.

These points, and Point Conception 30 miles farther southeast, are treacherous areas for ships and literally hundreds have foundered on their hidden shoals. At Point Conception I caught a glimpse of the white lighthouse tower behind some low lying buildings.

As the train sped eastward the Channel Islands came into view across the Santa Barbara Channel. Fishing trawlers plied the waters and gangs of pelicans nosedived around their nets. Again the lounge car came alive at this extraordinary sight.

At Gaviota Beach the train passes over a long tressel, a hundred feet above the creek and campgrounds. At Refugio Beach we looked up

Refugio Road to the Santa Ynez Mountains. On the ocean side campers and people on the beach waved as we raced by. Hitting 75 mph the train whipped through Goleta, then began the slow approach into Santa Barbara.

We left on time (2:17) and arrived nearly on time (4:35). My experienced family of riders said this was quite ordinary and expected of Amtrak, despite the jokes we hear about its tardiness. The next train back to San Luis Obispo was at 12:05 the next afternoon, so I had made arrangements to stay overnight.

I stepped out into strange territory. The 1905 mission style station was right in front of me and the historic Moreton Fig tree was to my left. Vicki, the Santa Barbara station agent, got me headed in the right direction to the Villa Rosa Inn; in less than five minutes I was comfortably tucked away in my temporary Santa Barbara home, ready to discover this city of exceptional beauty and intrique, but already looking forward to my return train trip.

Santa Barbara train station built in 1905.

3—Point Sal—
A Lonely Rugged Point
of Awesome Beauty

Point Sal is a headland of California coastline that has been a graveyard for many men and ships. Ships have blindly steamed into her jagged fogenshrouded cliffs, or miscalculated her hidden reef.

Far from any close harbor and nearly inaccessible from land, marooned ships foundered with little hope of being saved. The destruction was usually complete and on one occasion in 1876 Eliza Clark—who received Point Sal as a wedding gift from her father—gave a gold watch for the salvage rights to the schooner *Anna Lyle*. The salvaged ship's cabin became a school house for the small band of people engaged in a treacherous game of survival and shipping.

The Point had its heyday around 1875 when an 800-foot wharf serviced waiting ships. About 160 wagons a day plied the rough roads over the peaks to the wharf and to Chute Landing. The ships brought in tons of lumber for the first homes built in Central City (Santa Maria), and took away the produce of Guadalupe to San Francisco and other parts.

The residents called their little town Morrito. It had three homes, a post office, a general store, a blacksmith shop and a school. The coming of the narrow gauge railroad to Port San Luis (then Port Harford), brought stiff competition, and fierce winter storms had a way of undoing the wharf and making it flotsam. Today only a plateau with Monterey cedar, eucalyptus and a few artifacts gives a hint of a town site.

Point Sal's appeal today is its lonely beach and headlands. It's a paradise for adventurers willing to get out on a ledge above the frothing surf and experience the allure and savagery of a coast that both takes lives and enriches them.

Two miles south of Guadalupe along Route 1 is Brown Road. Bordered by anise this road runs nine miles west towards the ocean. After four miles there's a fork in the road to the El Corralitos Ranch. The road to the right is Point Sal Road, closed during bad weather or when Vandenberg Air Force Base is preparing a launch.

The road gets rougher and cars chatter on the washboard surface as it meanders over the hills. Tight hairpin turns on the steep grade soon give you an aerial perspective of the whole Santa Maria River basin. Still you're not on top.

At the crest of the hill there is a turn-out on the right side where hikers frequently stop to walk through the gate onto the privately-owned ridge road. The ridge road trail waves up and over rugged slopes to the Point, a walk of about three miles. From the numerous Chumash middens found along the ridge trail, it appears the Indians cherished this area, even though the point is often fog-bound and windswept.

The main road continues over the ridge, descending sharply 1200 feet to several parking areas above the 70-acre state beach. It's a lovely crescent-shaped beach with thunderous surf, surrounded by precipitous headlands of black basalt teetering toward the sea.

We walked the beach to the far north end until it ran up against a black igneous wall. Studying the 40-foot wall carefully, we discovered a spiraling series of toeholds, beginning at above the low tide mark. The high tide was in, so when the waves receded we dashed into the knee-high water to scamper onto the first ledge above the water. The rest of the way up was easy, so long as we didn't concentrate on the water sliding past the wall face below us.

On top the trail was faint but discernible. It traces the ledges above the water at distances of 10–30 feet, at times level and hard, then deeply pitched where alluvial fans of loose sand streamed across the path into the ocean. This is not a trail walk endorsed by the National Safety Council, but anyone with four feet and three hands ought to be able to handle it.

We crossed a short terrace that dropped 20 feet to a small beach. Previous hikers had planted a metal stake in the rock with a knotted rope descending to the lower level. We discovered the rappel down was easier than the return rappel upward.

Along the way we passed a half dozen small beaches that provided an exclusive Shangri-La for couples. Three deer bounded away like pogo sticks when we surprised them. A seal pup enjoying a beach all to himself looked amazed as we came into view, then decided we couldn't be trusted and wobbled into the surf where he studied us, studying him.

The barks of the seal herd on Lion Rock, several hundred yards off the Point, occupied our attention as we approached the end of our three-hour hike. Riding the waves like beach boys, playful seals curled and flipped in joyous confusion.

At the very end of Point Sal are two terraced protrusions high above the water that make ideal rest and lunch spots. To the north another long desolate beach stretched to the headlands of Mussel Point two miles away. Beyond Mussel Point the great Nipomo Dunes roll northward without interruption to Pismo Beach.

The temptation to hike onward to the (Guadalupe) Main Street beach, where we had left another vehicle, weakened as we imagined the time and energy required to complete such a strenuous trek (approximately four hours). We turned back.

The wind picked up as we completed our hike back to the car. A plowed sky of white furrows sliced the descending sun into crimson strata. The sea shimmered and waved back flaming reds until the horizon was lost and the sea and sky became one.

The gentleness of the day faded into a gray night of fog, sharp winds and chilling cold. A coyote stood on a high ridge above us watching our going. We would gladly give the land back to him. The lonely savagery of Point Sal guarantees him and all wild creatures a place they can call their own.

Go prepared. In warm weather take a quart of water per person for the hike. Shorts and tennis shoes are the best attire, but the weather is changeable so be prepared for chilling cold. There are no utilities or facilities at Point Sal State Beach.

Backpackers return from an overnight on Point Sal.

Docents reenact mission activities during Mission Life Day.

4—La Purisima Mission—Historic Gem Restored

It was the winter of 1821. The sun had set behind the Santa Ynez River and a cold blue sky cast an eerie light across the gardens and orchards of La Purisima Mission. It was the time of day when the oak trees appear black against the sky and all objects become apparitions.

In the campanarios the bells tolled the beginning of mass and the celebration of Christmas. The sound rolled across the grounds like fog, touching everyone and everything.

Two Indians outside the mission playing a traditional game like dice around a small fire stopped for a moment, then continued their game. Older children attending the kiln listened. Tonight was a special night. For a few hours at least they could get away to practice in the choir with the padre who was teaching them songs and chants.

A ghost-like ranchero on horseback appeared in the waning light, cantering past the orchard. The thudding hooves broke the silence as he hurried into the shelter of the mission walls where his wife and young child awaited him.

The night grew still. Life at the mission moved inside, warmed by candles and braziers crackling with the evening meal.

In the guest quarters the ranchero's wife was slapping corn tortillas into perfect rounds. Occasionally she would stop to listen for her horseman who had been gone long enough. Mission-made candles cast a mellowing glow around the white walls garlanded with strings of crimson peppers.

As the ranchero quartered his horse, the mission mule was brought in from a dizzying day's work of turning the grist mill. He and the horses would face mangers of hay while the bells tolled and a motley gang of Indian children in a Spanish mission sang Latin chants and 17th century Spanish motets.

The governor of the territory was in residence that night, occupying a large split room. To one side women and children chattered contentedly while the governor, alone, sat at a table seriously engrossed in the affairs of state.

The Franciscan Padre Payeras, too, was alone in his quarters. The concerns of earthquake, droughts, and epidemics were wearing him down. He looked like a man who was wondering why he hadn't chosen a contemplative life.

This is a scene reenacted by the docents of La Purisima Mission as part of their candlelight tour when they slip into 18th century garb, and assume for a moment the activities and customs of the mission's early residents. It is a dramatic depiction that remains deeply impressed in my memory.

Padre Payeras and nearly 1500 resident Indian neophytes survived a devasting earthquake in 1812 and built a totally new complex of buildings with 4½ foot thick walls and long corridors of fluted columns. The new site was on the north side of the Santa Ynez River along El Camino Real, nestled among oak trees on rolling countryside, close to water and protected from cool ocean breezes by a low mesa.

Their building continued through 1821 but ill winds began to blow. Mexico cranked up its revolution against Spain and the mission suffered from a shortage of money, credit and supplies. Strife between the Indians and the oppressive Spanish military led to an Indian revolt in 1823–24, with considerable bloodshed and executions.

By 1834 the long-expected secularization of the mission was decreed by the new Mexican governor and the possessions and assets of the mission were disbursed. In 1845 the mission and some of its land was sold for $1100 to Don Juan Temple of Los Angeles.

Over the years the mission was used variously to house sheep and cattle, a blacksmith shop and even a saloon. Vandals, scavengers and souvenir hunters removed doors, windows and roof tiles. Fully exposed to the elements, the mission melted like an ice cream cone on a hot summer day. Ceilings collapsed, walls became rounded vertical columns, and four feet of muddy adobe covered the floors.

In 1934 the Civilian Conservation Corps, under the careful direction of the National Park Service, began the exacting work of restoring the mission. The mission was dedicated as a state park on December 7, 1941, the day Japan bombed Pearl Harbor. Three major buildings had been reconstructed and in later years eight other buildings were brought back to life and use.

Visitors get involved in preparing the simple food of the mission.

The mission gets careful attention these days, now in the hands of the California State Park System and a company of loving docents who dote on her.

On December 8 the mission commemorates its 1787 founding, the celebrated date of the conception of Mary. The mission was named to honor Mary's holy birth. *Mission La Purisima Concepcion de Maria Santisima* translates into The Immaculate Conception of Most Holy Mary.

Three hundred luminaria light the way from the parking lot to the church and La Sala, a social gathering place of the mission. A selected choir presents a program of seasonal and period music in the candle-lit chapel, adorned with Christmas poinsettias. Following the concert everyone follows the lighted way to La Sala for refreshments of punch, coffee and cookies.

By five p.m. the gates and buildings close and all visitors leave the grounds. The gates will reopen at 6:15 for the seven p.m. celebration. Seating is limited so be on time, or you'll be listening to the concert on the outside.

It's free.

I have an idea that you may want to get to the mission mid-day for a tour of this outstanding facility. It is one of the largest restoration projects every undertaken in the U.S. A work force of 25-200 men worked continuously from 1934–1941.

There is also an annual fundraiser, a candlelight tour allowing visitors to observe the mission era activities I described earlier.

To get there take the Clark Street off ramp at Orcutt to Route 135 at the west end of town. Going south follow Route 1, Cabrillo Highway west toward Lompoc over some very winding, twisting roads. Turn left on Purisima Road, the first signal light following the yellow blinker at Burton Mesa Boulevard.

Nighttime driving is better on Highway S20, the road off Route 135 that goes to Vandenberg AFB. At Vandenberg, Highway S20 turns left and becomes Lompoc Casmalia Road. As it bisects Cabrillo Highway it becomes Purisima Road and runs past the mission.

5—Lompoc Flower Festival

Flower talk is heard a lot in June as Lompoc celebrates its Annual Flower Festival. On Saturday morning there is a floral float parade, recognized as one of the top five floral parades in California. In addition to the floral floats there are bands, marching and equestrian units, pretty girls and gobs of parade pageantry.

Events continue at Ryon Park with dozens of activities: flower displays, exhibits, art and craft booths, tours of flower fields, concerts and other entertainment.

Flower field tours are conducted on Saturday and Sunday afternoons beginning at Ryon Park, at O and Ocean Avenues. More than 1000 acres along a 19-mile drive exhibit 29 different bloomers. In the small plot near La Purisima Mission, for example, over 20 varieties are growing: Shasta daisies, coreopsis, candy tuft, shizanthus and myosotic (forget-me-not) and others.

I wondered how Lompoc became the Central Coast flower community.

Before there were sweet pea fields in Lompoc there were bean fields, and before that there was the La Purisima Mission, and before that was the Chumash Indian village of Lompo (stagnant water). In 1787 the Indian village situated along the Santa Ynez River "offered" free labor to build the mission and the mission became the center of trade and activity until 1834.

Following the mission came the farmers who found the valley good for bean seed production. In 1907 a bean farmer, Robert D. Rennie, was asked by an English grower to try producing sweet peas. He succeeded, superbly. Burpee Seed Co. in Philadelphia, which bought bean seed from Rennie, became interested in sweet peas and in 1920 Bodger and Denholm Seed Companies arrived. The first flower festival was held in 1922.

27

What the growers found ideal in the Lompoc-Santa Ynez River Valley were the constant ocean breezes, the small temperature fluctuations, a ten-month growing period and a dry harvest period from May through September.

One acre of sweet peas can produce 700–800 pounds of seed with over 250 seeds per ounce. One acre of marigolds can produce up to 250 pounds of seed with more than 2500 seeds per ounce.

All the growers operate greenhouses for controlled fertilizations and hybridizations, but the fields continue to produce varieties that don't require such strict supervision. Although a fair amount of seed production has been farmed out to South American subsidiaries of these companies, Lompoc holds on tightly to its title of flower child of the Central Coast.

If you want to hear festival flower talk, take Route 1 out of Santa Maria or Route 246 from Buelton to Lompoc and head for Ryon Park, at O and Ocean Avenues. The bus tours start here and information booths will direct you to the Alpha Club Accredited Flower Show and all the other events. The flower show is held in the Veteran's Memorial Building at H and Locust. Free bus service is provided from Ryon Park.

If you visit Lompoc for the festival, or any other event, be sure to include La Purisima Mission (See Chapter 4).

For further information on festival events, times and places call the Lompoc Chamber of Commerce, 736-4567, or the Lompoc Valley Festival Association, Inc., 735-8511.

New flower and vegetable varieties in Denholm Seed Company greenhouses.

Zaca Lake birdwatchers.

6—Zaca Lake—
Everybody's Secret Mountain
Lake Resort

Nobody was there when it happened, at least no one alive ever told the story. It was probably a cold winter night 80,000 years ago when the rain was coming in hard against the mountain. The earth quaked and a million tons of rock broke away from the canyon walls, sealing it off. Swollen creeks nervously fought their way to the sea through the boulders and debris, but the dam held. Swirling round and round, the tired waters came to rest in a lake of greath depth. That day Zaca Lake was born.

It's a jewel. It's one of the few natural lakes in southern California that maintains its water level throughout the year from underground springs. Streams originally filled it but a series of land slides and earthquakes sealed them off. Now no one is sure of the source of the water, but it's 58 feet deep and cobalt blue.

Actually it's not cobalt blue all year. There's a time in the winter when the surface waters become cooler and heavier than the bottom and the whole lake turns upside down. This massive churning causes great turbulence and dramatic color changes as the bottom sediment is stirred up. First the lake becomes milky gray, then turns shades of purple, magenta and pink. These whirlpools and sucking currents were spooky to the Chumash who gave the lake great spiritual significance and believed the lake was bottomless with another village of people living beyond.

As long as 8,000 years ago, the Oak Grove Tribe camped on the shores of Zaca Lake. Then 1,000 years ago the Chumash came to Zaca, the first resort owners in a long line of proprietors. Pictographs, gaming balls and bed-rock mortars indicate the Chumash came to bag frogs and turtles among the tules in the marshy lower lake, collect and grind the giant acorns of the valley oak and to hunt the deer in the surrounding woodland. They built their homes and boats of tules and had a "temescal," or sweat house, a prehistoric sauna bath that was used for physical and spiritual cleansing. They played "skinny," a game with balls, and did what most people do today—look across the water and fill themselves with the peace that passes understanding.

Nineteenth century conservationists appealed to Teddy Roosevelt to have Zaca Lake set aside as a national park, but that effort failed as did the state's last chance for ownership in 1947.

In 1895 John Libeu and his wife Catherine homesteaded 320 acres around Zaca Lake and kept open house for years for the many visitors who came up to eat Catherine's French delicacies of frog legs and squirrel pie and watch John ride his horse out on a sycamore limb where horse and rider would fall into the lake. John got around in the kitchen too. His advice for cooking the carp from the lake: "Fish must swim three times to be good—once in water, once in oil and finally in wine."

By 1927 all 320 acres became John Mitchell's; he built an elaborate BBQ area on the east side of the lake. It served well Los Rancheros Vistadores, the horsemen who traveled from ranch to ranch making merry and sleeping around campfires.

Charles "Pete" Jackson bought the whole caboodle in 1948 and built a group of handsome log cabins with stone fireplaces, and a wonderfully rustic lodge, all in use today, looking twice their age but in nearly perfect harmony with the natural history of Zaca.

The nonprofit Human Potential Foundation, dedicated to the expansion of human awareness bought Zaca in 1985 with ambitious plans for development. But thirteen deer grazing in a canyon meadow, geese on the pond, and Ruby Crowned Kinglets and other LBJ's (little brown jobs) flitting through the bush just don't state this is a high-powered commercial enterprise.

In fact, this place is so laid back I felt over-dressed in tennis shoes, denim pants and a wool sweater. When I walked into the lodge a stereo system was sitting on a table flexing its watts, belting out Merle Haggard's *I'm Just An Okie From Muskogee*. Behind the reception desk a hired hand, looking like a cattle rustler, offered his help.

The dining room is homey and rustic with hand-made chairs and tables. The floor sags graciously (or is it decrepitly?) toward the water and large bay windows overlook the big, old sycamore trees where Libeu used to ride his horse.

The restaurant serves hearty meals for visitors and overnight guests. Coming up for lunch or supper, or for a drink, is a great idea if you can't stay over, but call ahead if you're going to be late. They go to bed early if customers aren't in sight.

The walk around the 30-acre lake is idyllic. The north-facing walls of the mountains are rich in trees, with pockets of color from the big leaf maples, while the south-facing slopes are barren and exposed. It's a favorite place for bird watchers, nature loves and people lovers. Mary Gosselin and her husband came up here mid-week on their tenth wedding anniversary, swam out to the raft with a bottle of French wine and toasted themselves and everyone else who came down the road.

Picnic facilities, swimming, pedal boating, canoeing and fishing make Zaca Lake ideal for day use. There are also trails from Zaca Lake into the back country and to Zaca Peak Road, Zaca Ridge Road and Catway Road. Fully-furnished cabins with Jacuzzis and fireplaces make it attractive for extended stays. (Call for current rates.) There's even a tennis court next to John Libeu's 80-year-old orchard.

'Can't think of a better way to spend an Indian summer day than to open a cabin door on to a grassy slope overlooking sparkling water. You might fall right off your rocker if you see the Rolling Stones, the Beach Boys or Paul Newman, all of whom recently visited here. It's everybody's secret. Shh . . .

Two ways to get there. The easy way is to take Route 101 to Zaca Station Road, 500 yards north of Route 154 to San Marcos Pass. Turn left and go 5.5 miles beyond the Firestone Winery over the grade to the entrance to Zaca Lake Resort. Drive the 7 miles through ranch land and across the meandering Zaca Creek (5 times) to the narrowing of the canyon where you climb the 20° grade. Stick it in first for the tight switch-back climb to the top. At 2400 feet you'll first come to a small pond and around the next curve the 30-acre lake shimmering in the sun.

A more adventurous way is to exit east on Betteravia Road (Route 176) in Santa Maria, which runs through the little towns of Garey and Sisquoc. At Sisquoc turn left on Foxen Canyon Road and parallel the Sisquoc River through the produce fields and vineyards. A mile beyond Zaca Mesa Winery on the left side of the road is the entrance to Zaca Lake.

Returning from Zaca Lake one evening we followed Zaca Station Road to the Zaca Creek Restaurant, a mile north of Buellton on Route 101. It's a dynamic place where bells clang and handsome waitresses hustle out he-man portions of steaks and fresh fish. The whole affair is well done. Try their Zaca Coca Roca dessert. It's unforgettable.

For information and reservations write or call. Zaca Lake Resort, P.O. Box 187, Los Olivos, 93441. Ph. 688-4891.

The peacock's fresh at the Circle Bar B.

Barbecue pit at the Circle Bar B.

7—Circle Bar B—
Back Country Horseback Riding
and Dinner Theater

We followed a huge bus off Route 101, near Goleta, onto Refugio Beach Road. The road turned east under the freeway and coursed through citrus and avocado groves. The matronly bus had a dickens of a time negotiating the tight turns on a road that was getting narrower and hillier.

This is the route the Queen of England followed in a jeep in 1983 when she came in the rain to visit President Reagan. Rancho del Cielo, the President's western retreat, is up Refugio Road, about six miles from the beach, but all you can see is a stone-pillared entrance with the name Duos Vistos and a battery of electronic eyes around an unmanned guard house.

I felt assured that if a busload of people from Los Angeles was coming up this road for an evening of fun we were on the right track.

The Circle Bar B Dinner Theater is so unusual I find it hard to describe. My friend said it reminded her of an open air Italian picnic ground, situated among old Girl Scout cabins. I thought it might have been designed by a committee of 17 who never talked to each other.

One designer placed the parking lot at the far end of a maze that wanders in and out of horse corrals. I felt like I was going in for a load of manure; but pushing on and following handmade signs tacked to posts and gates, I found the company of Volvos, Fords and Peugeots in a grassy lot. Another designer thought that flying peacocks at mealtime would be nice. So what if there's a few feathers in your beer and another bird on the ground stalking your dinner? All the designers agreed that if a restful country atmosphere is going to be achieved, straight lines and logical organization should be avoided at all costs.

If I wasn't so amused and charmed by the Circle Bar B, I'd call it a parody. It's Florence Brown's old (1941) 1000 acre girls' camp which became a family ranch and later a home for Santa Barbara's theatrical talent. Rustic cabins and verandas overhung with lattice work and grapevines make this place the quintessential *laissez faire* California hideaway.

During the daytime, ranch guests sit around the pool or walk among the horses in an atmosphere that is like a stopped moment in time. But around 6:30 the dust begins to swirl as guests arrive for the scrumptious outdoor barbecue.

Any Friday or Saturday night and Sunday afternoon, you can have a top rate tri-tip barbecue dinner, including several salads, bread, dessert and beverage, followed by barn theater. Sunday brunch features Cornish game hens, vegetables, rolls, salads, quiche, juice and champagne. Dinner theater rates are $25 while overnight guests pay $128 (for two) for a rustic room, all meals, or $186 for a stay in one of their new cabins which are complete with king beds, fireplaces, and redwood decks.

Dinner is served on an open porch, shaded by towering trees and canopies of grapevines. Peacocks strut among the tables scrounging for handouts and dropped morsels. When a squabble broke out between them, the routed bird flew like a broom over the tables, trailing himself across salads and medium rare. Nobody seemed to mind. In fact they applauded.

After supper we strolled across the grounds, past the ubiquitous horses and stables, to a converted farm building—the theater. It seats 90+ people which through the years has been improved to include tiered seating, air conditioning and professional staging and lighting. The playbill features the likes of "Tintypes," "The Seven-Year Itch," and "It Had To Be You."

For $23 you can ride for 1.5 hours along trails that traverse high ridges with views toward the Channel Islands. There are also 2.5 hour rides ($40) and half day trips ($50) to romantic groves and picturesque streams. My friend and I jockeyed for positions as we ran along the ridge, but then stopped to drink in the immensity of these mountains. As the trail descends it goes by a set of waterfalls. At one point a double strand of yellow rope marks a thickety trail where lovers can rappel down to a quiet pool. The horse ride is a pleasant way to get ready for the dinner theater. Nothing like a day in the saddle followed by supper at the old chuck wagon with entertainment around the camp fire.

If you're just out for a drive up Refugio Road, stop when you hear the call of the peacocks. It's show time at the Circle Bar B, and an experience you won't forget.

For show reservations call (805) 965-9563, or 968-1113 if you plan to stay overnight.

A hearty ranch-style barbecue at the Circle Bar B.

Back country hot springs are usually rock and clay bathing holes.

8—Gaviota Hot Springs— Indian Bathing Hole in Los Padres National Forest

The Santa Ynez Mountains look like a huge spiney dinosaur stretching east to west, from Santa Barbara to Point Conception. The ocean is on the south side and the Santa Ynez Valley on the north. Peaks of 4300 feet have been thrust upward from compression along the Santa Ynez fault line.

Somewhere in these mountains there was a back country hot springs that I had heard about.

We stopped along the way for directions to the springs, but as often happens the locals didn't know where it was. A few more clues had us traveling south along Route 101, passing Buellton and getting off at Route 1. We turned up the ramp as if going to Lompoc, but at the stop sign at the top of the ramp, turned left and crossed over Route 101, then right onto a frontage road that runs parallel to the freeway.

In a quarter mile there's a sign that boldly announces "Gaviota State Park Hot Springs Parking Area." I wondered how this spot had remained such a secret.

We parked the car and trudged up a dirt road that ascends sharply towards the hot springs. In a quarter mile we passed a jeep trail off to the right, that we discovered later totally encircles Gaviota Peak, the 2450-foot crown which overlooks Gaviota Pass and the country around. We stayed with the main trail which veers left.

A quarter mile up the foot trail we came to another fork. Going to the right we spotted a large green palm. An oasis. At least an indication of a water hole. As we approached closer we saw a large sycamore over-hanging two pools, one terraced above the other. Hot springs are fairly

39

common in California but finding one in the back country is a thrill. Water that fell many years ago has run a mysterious course through the heated interior of the earth. Then there it is: water gurgling to the surface through 35-million-year-old marine sea bed rock.

The springs at Gaviota (also called Las Cruces) are unusual inasmuch as tritium dating shows the water to be about 38 years old, coming from a depth of about 3280 feet, with water temperature of 115°F and a rate of flow of 25 gallons a minute. (Each spring has its own depth and recirculation time so generalities to other springs don't apply, but may be close.)

Totally submersed in the upper pool three people, faces caked in clay, watched us. Except for round eyes and pink mouths they were slate gray, with patches of the stuff drying on their cheek bones and forehead. I thought we had found some aboriginal Californians.

Their clothes lay in piles on the rocks in front of the pools. I didn't know what was most interesting, the collection of clothing items strewn about or those weird faces in the water.

"How's the water?" (The stock question.)

"Fine, c'mon in." (I could have guessed.)

I wasn't so sure I wanted to. Gaviota Hot Springs is not a finished bath with tile walls and ledges. It's a bathing hole, sculptured by flowing water and ages of people who have found respite in a warm bath on a hillside.

The upper pool is the warmest. Water ripples down from the source into the pool, clear as water can be, but the fine particle clay sides stirred up by human activity gives it the appearance of wash water. If you are the first to arrive, the pools are clear and quiet.

First the big toe, then the foot. Soon I was in up to my neck feeling the warmth . . . doing nothing but sitting there listening to the music of the spheres.

After a good soaking we headed up a trail leading from the hot springs to the top of the ridge. It's a heart-thumping 1½ hours to the top on a service road. After a series of ascending knolls we were in the clouds and on top of Gaviota Peak, at an elevation of 2450 feet. Our reward for the climb was a breaktaking view of Point Conception, Gaviota Pass just below, and the Channel Islands off to the south.

The trail continues along in a westerly direction, then descends and loops north past some interesting caves until it circles full around and intersects the trail that we had hiked to the springs.

The trails are even and smooth, and lightweight shoes are fine. Take water. The hot springs are closed at sunset, so make it a daytime experience.

A digression ... There is a ridge top road that undulates continuously over the Santa Ynez Mountains from Gaviota to Santa Barbara. The ridge road-hiking trail, called Camino Cielo, is closed to vehicular traffic between Gaviota Peak and Refugio Road where it ambles past President Reagan's ranch.

East of Refugio, Camino Cielo continues as an all-weather dirt road to San Marcos Pass and beyond. The section east of San Marcos Pass is particularly scenic, with aerial views of Santa Barbara and north into the San Rafael Wilderness.

There are two other back country hot mineral baths along this eastern leg of Camino Cielo. Big Caliente Hot Springs is a National Forest-developed bath with change rooms and a structured pool. Little Caliente, off the trail, is an undeveloped natural bath.

To get to these two baths take Route 154 to San Marcos Pass, then turn left (east) onto East Camino Cielo at the top of the pass. This road is paved for most of its length.

An ancient Indian hot tub is a pleasant place to spend a lazy afternoon.

Rider overlooks the Cuyama badlands.

9—Sespe-Frazier Wilderness— Overnight Horseback Trip With a Mountain Man

Someone told me about a mountain man in the Sespe-Frazier Wilderness Area, just south of here who sleeps with his horses, howls in the moonlight with his dogs, and has such a love for nature he forgets to come home.

I wanted to meet this guy so I dialed his number. A recorded voice came on . . . "Howdy, pardner. I know you're calling to talk to Pardner; well, all of us cowboys call each other that. It's just a Chorro Grande Pack Station way of saying, 'Hello.' We're looking forward to seeing all you buckaroos and buckarettes, so squeeze into your jeans, pull on your boots and get on up here for a fine mountain good time. If this is you, Dale, tell Roy we found his horse."

So I squeezed into my jeans and pulled on my boots to see what this was all about. I drove to Santa Maria, then headed east on Highway 166 toward Maricopa. At Cuyama I picked up Route 33 and headed east, past the Pine Mountain turnout.

Pardner Hicks lives on a ranch in a little story-book house made of logs and mortar, on Route 33 between Cuyama and Ojai. It's the old Frank Felt home. Felt, a mountain man and poet, came into this wilderness in 1918 to recuperate from war wounds, and stayed for 50 years, bequeathing his poetry and his home to Pardner who assumes the task of sharing it with everyone who visits.

Pardner does what he does best. He takes city slickers into the back country on horseback and shows them the life of wranglers and mountain men.

Our two-day trip into California Condor country began in the corral as strangers shook hands and horses were brought to the tack shed for blankets, saddles and packs. Pardner talked to each horse affectionately as he readied them for the ride. Every person was matched to a horse,

43

and a relationship between man and beast began even before the corral gate opened.

On the trail, horse and rider became one; two warm-blooded animals communicating with each other by sound and touch, developing a bond of friendship and trust that grew with every steep descent and creek crossing.

The trail meandered through bushy groves of willow along the creek, then through a thicket where rose hips beamed like Christmas berries. The happy dogs bounded in and out of the chaparral smelling a world of intoxicating odors and chasing every scampering lizard. Fragrances of aromatic herbs washed over us as we plodded along through Yerba Santa and Mormon Tea.

Our ascent to the 8000-foot mountains began along monolithic sandstone formations and across streams where Pardner's panting dogs rushed in to cool off. Like crocodiles, they laid in the water, bodies totally submersed with only their heads lying on the surface.

Horses strained. Men leaned into the motion, trying to make a rhythm with the rocking horse. Dark clouds covered the sun and the disposition of the group changed to gray.

At 6000 feet we came to a white bark fir. The air was cool. Then the Jeffrey pines and sugar pines appeared. The strands became denser and the trees bigger. Thunder grumbled . . . then tapered off to silence. The horses shuffled on. Then with a flash and a clap the thunder started again, repeating its growling until it let loose a gentle drizzle.

Misty rain filtered the dust and made the air smell wet. As we approached our camp, the drizzle became a shower and we quickly tied up our horses to scurry for shelter under large boulders on the hillside.

Lying on a soft litter of pine needles in the shadow of a boulder in the rain, I realized there were no defenses or barriers between us and the earth.

The sodden sky broke. Rain gave way to ethereal steam rising from the warm earth. Men came from under rocks and Kevin, Pardner's right-hand man, began a fire with materials that loathed the thought of kindling. Heavy smoke lazed about while horses rested and Pardner began movements that suggested supper was on its way.

Pardner sets a table from the bounty of his garden—fresh squash, corn on the cob and salad, accompanying thick steaks and spaghetti. Hot chocolate and camp coffee washed over it in a happy mix that stomachs knowingly identify as a picnic or holiday.

Around a glowing campfire we sat with sated bellies and drowsy eyes while Pardner read the poetry of Frank Felt . . . proverbial things like:

Possess little and you are spared the sorrow of its
loss.

Sleeping under the stars was easy. On a two-inch mat of needles,
under a cloudless sky I watched a shooting star, and then traced the path
of a satellite across the black. In the distance Ventura twinkled like a
constellation.

Sleepers stayed in their sacks until the sun pulled them out. By that
time Kevin had made another smokey fire and blended in the aromas of
coffee and bacon until we couldn't resist any longer.

We ate a breakfast suited for cowhands who had just driven 10,000
longhorns from Montana to California. I was even beginning to swagger
like a cowboy.

The ride after breakfast was along the craggy mountain ridges overlooking the Cuyama Badlands, home to Three-Fingered Jack and Joaquin Murietta when they plundered the early Californians and hid suc-
cessfully in land pushed together like folds in poured cake batter.

The trail moved through groves of mature pine and spruce to overlooks across chasms of thousands of feet. Pardner answered our questions about trees and condors and gave answers to questions we hadn't
even thought of, until we knew the land like a friend.

We broke camp around noon and put our bulky objects on the truck
that Kevin drove back to the ranch. His horse returned with us, running
riderless along with the dogs, enjoying the liberty of stopping to muzzle
some good grass, then galloping to catch up.

For riders and horses going back was a silent time. Nothing more
to say or do. We had been to the mountains, and we had changed some-
what. The horses and the dogs and camaraderie were difficult to leave
behind.

Several years ago Pardner turned his business over to Tony Alvis'
Los Padres Wilderness Outfitters.

Tony has spent a lifetime in the Sespe wilderness, riding in the
shadow of the giant California condors before the time of their extinction.
He knows the Indian caves where early men painted pictures on rocks;
he leads people to the back country hot springs, cooks gourmet meals
around campfires and puts people to bed under constellations of stars.
Day trips or extended two to seven day trips can be arranged.

Tony is a horseshoer, blacksmith, nature lover and artist. He's a
cowboy who is thoroughly competent and authentically rugged.

Call Los Padres Wilderness Outfitters for information: (805) 648-
2113.

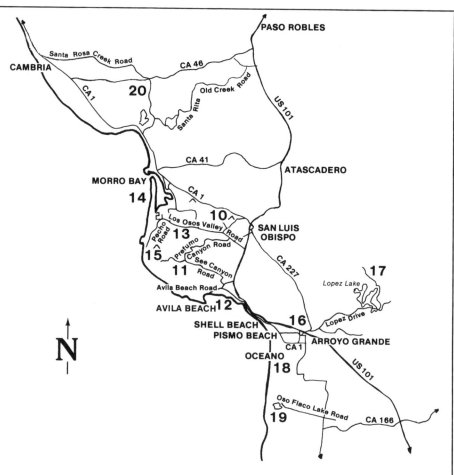

10 Bishop's Peak
11 Irish Hills
12 Hot Springs at Avila and Sycamore
13 Los Osos Oaks Reserve
14 Exploring Morro Bay Sand Spit
15 Valencia Peak
16 Arroyo Grande Bicycle Tour
17 Big and Little Falls
18 Horseback Riding the Beaches and
   Back Dunes of Oceano
19 Coreopsis Hill Hike
20 Motorcycling the Back Roads From
   Pismo Beach to Cambria

II In the Heart
of the Central Coast

Bishop Peak overlooks the northwest edge of San Luis Obispo.

10—Bishop's Peak—
A High Way to See SLO City

At the close of a day I sat on the side of Bishop Peak. The hikers were all down, the turkey vultures had ceased their endless aerial turns and the city was tucking itself in for the night. The scene was as quiet as a picture.

Far below kids turned up driveways into suburban homes and doors closed on the fading light. Across the ravine a bellicose cow mooed while its sisters stood as still as figurines.

I wondered what Cabrillo thought when he came this way in 1582 and named the big rock standing in the bay "El Moro." Looking into the valley of the bears he could see seven peaks, all in a row, with broad valleys on either side.

With no billboards or highway signs I imagine the mountain peaks were read like a map. Many of the early explorers and settlers talked about the "Seven Sisters" or "Morros."

What makes this string of peaks so fascinating is that they are distinctly different than the other mountains around them. For years geologists and students have been staring at these peaks, walking across them, and chipping away at them. The conclusion? They're ancient volcanic domes or remnants of intrusive plugs, 23 million years old. All around are sedimentary mountain ranges that are youngsters of only one million years. Geologists conclude the plugs were formed at great depths and later thrust up and exposed by erosion.

The dacite granite rock of the peaks is fine-grained and very hard; so despite some fissures and cleavages, they are standing firm, resisting the wear and tear that comes with the wind and the rain.

The first of these peaks is Islay, at 775 feet, situated east of the San Luis Obispo County Airport. It has a beacon on it. Then comes San Luis

49

Mountain at 1292 feet, with a road scar across it and the Madonna Inn at its base. Across Foothill Boulevard is Bishop Peak, 1559 feet, named by the padres at the mission because the three points on the peak resemble the headpiece of Bishop Saint Louis (San Luis). Farther west is Chumash, 1257 feet, then the bold head of Cerro Romaldo, 1306 feet.

Approaching Morro Bay is Hollister Peak, 1404 feet, conspicuous in its masterful size; then Cabrillo, 971 feet, and finally Black Hill, 665 feet, overlooking South Bay Boulevard. Standing up to its knees in water is Morro Rock at 581 feet. That makes *nine* Seven Sisters. There's a tenth—the Davidson Sea Mount—completely submersed. It was discovered by a survey ship in 1932.

The peaks were all privately-owned at one time but in 1980 150 acres of Bishop Peak were donated to the California State Parks Foundation. Black Hill, parts of Chumash and Cerro Romaldo are also under state jurisdiction. Public-minded groups have long advocated a linear park system including all the peaks from San Luis Obispo to Morro Bay.

The most popular approach to Bishop Peak is from Foothill Boulevard, about .4 mile south of Patricia Drive, or 1.3 miles north of O'Connor Way; near the Calvary Baptist Church and a creek there is a turnout that accommodates about 20 cars. Another approach is off the end of Patricia Drive.

Either way slip between or under the barbed wire and say hello to the Herefords that are grazing on the green foothill slopes. The walk up the grassy hill is gradual with lots of chips to kick. Stick to the worn paths; it's easier. Don't forget to take water and a snack. When you near the grove of oaks, you can decide if you came for a picnic or a hike.

Beyond the groves of trees the trails become less obvious and very steep. It's sweat and grunt from there to the top, but small children and adults of all ages make it, so you can too. The large granite boulders are smooth and round . . . very slippery when dusted with a bit of soil. Watch your footing. Coming down can be trickier than going up.

Once on top you will be rewarded with views of the Oceano Dunes, Point Sal and the piney hills of Cambria. Bishop Peak towers above the rest of the Morros affording an exquisitive view to Morro Rock in the misty far away.

On the Los Osos Valley side of Bishop Peak, you can see a mean gouge out of the mountain's hide where quarrying provided building stones for the Presbyterian Church, the County Historical Society building, and other early-day projects. The big "B" (Bishop) on the Chorro Valley side of the mountain marks an area of some old mining activity and a place of idyllic grassy savannas, great for lunching, flying kites or simply lazing in the sun. Get there from Patricia Drive.

Because the foothills to these beautiful peaks are privately owned, take along a grateful attitude for the owners who allow us access to the peaks. Walk gently and carry a smile.

Some come to hike to the summit; some come to picnic below.

Atop the Irish Hills Amy and Alan look over green hills toward San Luis Obispo.

11—Irish Hills—
The Long Way Home

It isn't everyday that I get a chance to be alone with Thelma, so I took advantage of the situation.

She had been to the orthopedic surgeon in San Luis; and when I picked her up at the front door of the clinic, I said in my most charming manner, "Shall we take the long way home, Thelma?"

"How long is long?" she quipped.

"About an hour," I said, "but the Irish Hills above Avila ought to be living up to their name after the wonderful rains we've been having."

"OK, you're the driver. Take me for a ride."

So, I did.

The road across the Irish Hills begins in San Luis Obispo off Los Osos Valley Road on Prefumo Canyon Road—about a half mile west of Madonna Road.

Prefumo begins as an ordinary city street, running through a neighborhood of tract condominiums, but soon turns into a tight twisting (barely) two-lane road as it winds up into the Irish Hills, then curls back down through See Canyon on the other side, connecting with the road to Avila Beach.

A large yellow sign shouts WINDING ROAD NEXT 13 MILES— and then another sign warns—NOT ADVISABLE IN WET WEATHER.

The road winds in and out of the rising canyon, past little ranchos and along picket fences of rustic homes with smoke curling from fireplace chimneys. There are many idyllic spots where runners and motorists stop.

Roland and Patti stood in an entangled embrace alongside the road, their bikes lying about them like they had been dumped in a reckless moment of passion. If I had lowered my window, I could have heard Roland ask Patti to marry him.

The canyon is that kind of place; and the higher you get the harder you breathe. The air gets thin, the head gets light, smiles become giggles and before you know it something foolish happens.

We continued along the stream where giant sycamores stand and willows show off their pussy willow catkins. After about five miles the open grasslands of the Irish Hills appear and the brushy stream bed habitat is left behind.

The road wraps around the hills like a ribbon, at times perilously narrow and close to the edge. There have been more than a few encounters between little zippy cars and broad-beamed Detroit models sprawled across the lanes. Their meeting is painful, embarrassing and a long way from the nearest garage. The tow truck driver often falls into a trance when he sees cars in the ditch along this section and only the sight or smell of a $20 bill brings him to his senses again.

But if you're careful you'll smell the real green of spring, and see the outburst of flowers that makes this area unique. Nearly every species of flowers in the tri-county area is found on these hills, making it mecca for botanists and wildflower lovers.

At the summit are stupendous views northwest over Morro Bay and the magnificent volcanic morros. On a dark night the light at Piedras Blancas can be seen. To the south we could look into Shell Beach and Pismo. Thelma said that in all her 80 years she had never seen this, though she had been up See Canyon from the Avila side a few times.

Albert Barre tells me the McHenrys, McArdles and McAndees came to this area in the 1880s and named it the Irish Hills. Francis McArdle deeded his land to George Johe in 1892, and George's daughter, Lizzie, married a Frenchman, Edward Barre, who bought out his father-in-law. Lizzie bore seven children up in the cream-colored Victorian bungalow that faces the road next to the Texas longhorn corral. Edward raised dairy cows and brought the cream down to the L.A. Creamery by horse and wagon (where Foster Freeze is now, on Marsh Street).

Albert Barre, one of the sons, took over the farm in 1935, and milked 40 head. He made daily trips to the Golden State Creamery on Higuera, now The Creamery shopping plaza.

Today the farm is the home of "Tex," the Cal Poly-raised longhorn steer and 99 of his fellow kind that roam the open range on top. They're wonderfully adapted animals, having survived in the American wilderness since their escape from the Spaniards and mission padres coming out of Mexico in the 17th century.

The longhorns eat poison oak, have 100 per cent calving rates, run like horses, endure drought, and have intelligence and wit that make herefords look like dolts. On one hill we watched a matronly cow tend seven calves, while their mothers grazed 100 feet away in a large circle of protection.

The road goes through to the other side and we began to wind down into See Canyon. Recent rains had washed huge boulders and tons of gravely canyon wall onto the road but we could squirm through.

See Canyon is a unique cold-air canyon. Shielded from the low-lying winter sun the canyon has long cold spells that makes for ideal flowering conditions. The variety of apples in the canyon is dependent on the extent and duration of the cold periods. The trees bloom in April and May and make a beautiful spectacle.

Visit the canyon then, and return in late summer and fall, for shopping among the small orchards that offer great varities of wonderful edibles and fresh cider.

Thelma liked it. It took her 80 years to get up over the top and down the other side. I hope it doesn't take you that long.

Prefumo Canyon Road leads up to views of hilly grasslands as green as Ireland's.

Most tubs are small, but El Grande is big enough for a company party.

12—Hot Springs at Avila and Sycamore

You say your relatives are coming to visit this summer and you don't want to drive all over the state to entertain them? Fine.

Within ten miles of San Luis Obispo you can fish off a pier, have supper at the ocean's edge, walk a sandy beach, horseback ride the cliffs over San Luis Bay or soak in hot mineral baths and tubs at Avila Hot Springs and Sycamore Mineral Springs.

Avila Beach was a popular area with the smugglers who came into Pirates Cove during Prohibition, bringing their precious cargo of booze to Avila Hot Springs for distribution to San Francisco and Los Angeles.

Travelers to Hearst Castle also found Avila Hot Springs a full service speak-easy. One patron left behind a large Victorian mirror which still stands in the lobby. The Hot Springs began in 1907 when the first owners drilled for oil, but at 900 feet hit hot water instead. The oil at 3000 feet didn't bring great rewards so a row of mineral baths was built around the well head in a building that you can see today. A few years later the pool was added, with a kiddies' pool off to the side.

Robert and Paula Snowdy bought Avila Hot Springs in 1969, put in a first class RV park and purged the place of its seamy past. Many renovation changes have taken place and it appeals now to lap swimmers and families looking for good clean fun.

The hot mineral baths are clean and freshly painted, the tepid swimming pool is crystal clear and the kiddies' pool has been converted to a lounging hot pool for all ages, with the 130 degree mineral spring water cooled down to 105 degrees—hot enough to make a steamy aura about you when you step out on a cool night.

Eighty-four-year-old Paul Bedrosian has been coming to Avila for 15 years, drinking the mineral water and swimming six laps every day.

He has logged 750 miles in that time and he'll qualify, along with others on the board for a certificate and patch from the American Red Cross for his accomplishments of fitness.

If you don't swim, here's the place to learn. The comfortably warm 86 degree water and licensed swimming instructors will help you create a good lifelong habit.

Only a fraction of the population has ever had a massage, a service closely associated with mineral spas.

It's a wonderfully indulgent experience and expertly performed by three women and two men massage therapists at Avila Hot Springs. Many have graduated from Santa Barbara's Institute for Holistic Studies, which stresses the therapeutic quality of massage.

I learned to talk about energy centers, acupressure, meridians, lymphatics and the emotional release that often accompanies the massage. Then my masseuse went to work, kneading my body with buttery soft hands until all the knots had dissipated into euphoric relaxation. The head and face manipulation was the finale, and I believe I heard angels softly singing. I was transcended.

For $40 an hour, or $25 for a half hour, you too can take this great trip. A hot mineral bath or a swim is a good way to get ready for the massage. Call 595-2359 for an appointment.

Avila Hot Springs is open until midnight during the summer months and shows old time movies in the shallow hot pool. *Laurel and Hardy* are popular and *Jaws* has been known to empty the pool. Excellent hamburgers and drinks are available and a game room and pool table caters to a wide range of ages and interests.

Sycamore Mineral Springs, around the corner from Avila Hot Springs, on Avila Beach Road, had a different beginning. It began as a health resort, with three small hotels housing 200 guests. Formal gardens, a fine restaurant, swimming pool, mineral baths and attendants in white coats catered to the people who came for the treatment of arthritis, asthma and everything else.

In the late '20s the Depression hit, and the resort was leased to the Civilian Conservation Corps. Today Sycamore is making a comeback as a mineral spring and therapeutic massage resort. Twenty-six motel units feature acrylic spas on their porches and 24 honeymoon cottages with spas and fireplaces are planned along San Luis Creek. Four masseuse and masseurs are on staff.

What most people come to Sycamore for is the opportunity to use the redwood tubs placed on ledges and up steep staircases on the hills above the main building.

Most of the tubs are 500 gallons, suitable for two to six people, but one is El Grande, good for up to 50. During "WOW" week at Cal Poly, fraternities and sororities fill El Grande with rubber duckies and freshmen initiates for a frolicking baptism into "Greek" collegiate life.

For $9.50 per person/hour you can enjoy tubbing under the oaks and sycamores. Some of the tubs have complete decking and enclosures for privacy. Three women came in at noon with a picnic basket. At tub side they spread out their delectables and floated along their homespun smorgasbord, snacking and giggling, snacking and gossiping.

The tubs are used frequently in the morning and early afternoon, but sunset is a special time when a peach-colored sky, dusky with fog rolling in over the Avila hills creates enchanting silhouettes of oak tree limbs in lacey bonsai shapes.

The landscape view fades imperceptibly until stars and the moon peep through the gnarly canopy.

The tubs all have names—Rendezvous, Twilight, Enchantment, Tubby, Hideaway, Shangri-la, Cove, Deja-vu and 18 others.

Try *Tubby* if you want total privacy, *Shangri-la* if you want quiet and openness, and *Enchantment* if you want a deep woods environment.

Some things to take along... a bottle of chilled wine, some exquisite canapes, a candle and holder, a strolling violinist... and the confidence you'll have a good time.

Avila Hot Springs is adjacent to Route 101 on Avila Beach Road. Phone 595-2359. Sycamore Mineral Springs is one-half mile west of Route 1001 on Avila Beach Road. Phone 595-7302 or 1-800-234-5831 for reservations.

The 86° water of the Avila Hot Springs pool allows year-round swimming.

Docent Tom White often leads hikes through the Oaks Reserve.

13—Los Osos Oaks Reserve—
An Ancient Grove Tells a Story

The Chumash Indians never learned to use the golden grizzly bear for food. The bears were tough to kill, so man and beast lived together in some kind of truce with occasional casualties on both sides.

The Spanish conquistadores had a lethal approach—guns, lariats, lances and horses—all the tools necessary to corral the quarry and put them away.

Don Gaspar de Portola and his troops came through our county in 1769 and went on to discover Monterey. In 1771, while still up north, his hungry band of 63 men suffered a famine. Remembering the large number of bears seen in the Los Osos Valley, Portola sent 70 ox-drawn wagons south into the valley to hunt for bear. This expedition bagged over 100 bears and headed back up north with over 9000 pounds of bear jerky.

By 1850 or '60 a few bears were still around in Los Osos Valley, but these were but a few stragglers looking for a mate. The end was in sight and these last bears satisfied our curiosity for something strange. They appeared in rodeos, in cages and in staged bear fights. After 1860 there were no more.

These tales and more come to mind as you walk the Los Osos Oaks State Reserve, a 90-acre preserve of oaks and chaparral on Los Osos Valley Road. It represents the kind of habitat in the valley that has flourished for thousands of years—a home for the Chumash and the bears.

As I entered the grove of coast live oaks from Los Osos Valley Road, I felt the transformation from the clatter of roadway and machines to the greenhouse ambience of the tree's canopy. In a damp hollow near the creek, a class of kids sat in the limbs of one of the old giants, like birds on a branch, eating their lunch. They were as quiet as mushrooms, watching me walk on the soft duff of the forest floor.

In 1910 Shorty expressed his love for Leona with a carving in the trunk of the tree the kids were sitting in. It reminded me of a tatoo that grows on a fat man. Too bad, Shorty. Your message of love is an ugly scar, magnified by time.

The oaks reserve was once a moving dune, at the time of the last ice age 10,000 years ago. Since then dune grasses and chaparral have moved in and stablized things. When the humus was sufficient, acorns germinated and grew up, eventually spreading their seeds up and down the slopes.

There's a 250-foot rise from the roadside entrance and creek bottom to the top of the old dunes. Along the ascending trail there is a concert grove of gnarled trees, with interlocking arms overspreading a sylvan amphitheater. It's an idyllic woodland spot for Mozart festival concerts of woodwinds and strings, and a living laboratory for countless natural history classes that gather here.

As I crested the old dunes, I saw minikin oak trees, as old as their 800-year-old relatives down by the roadside and creek. Here, struggling against the salty wind and dry soil, they grow as natural bonsai trees, shaped by the hardships of life at the top.

Gauzy lichens hang down from the trees. The loosely woven strands of algae and fungus were just right for use as compresses and diapers by the Indians.

Nearby chips of chert and fragments of shells suggest the location of an old Indian campsite. Tom White, a museum docent, thinks this was probably a temporary site, with major village sites being at the mouth of Morro Bay, near Spooner's ranch house in Montana De Oro and near the San Luis Bay Inn at Avila.

Thanks to the efforts of Emily Polk and Dart Industries who provided half the funds to acquire the land as a preserve, the inevitable progression of native land to housing tracts was halted. Instead of another trailer park we're able to walk in old dunes where ancient trees spread their branches overhead.

To get there take Los Osos Valley Road into Los Osos. Near the Baptist Church is a parking area for the preserve on the south side of the road (¾ mile east of South Bay Boulevard). Catch a walk with one of the docents of the Natural History Museum of Morro Bay State Park; the enthusiastic docents are full of good information. A weekly listing of docent walks is published in county newspapers.

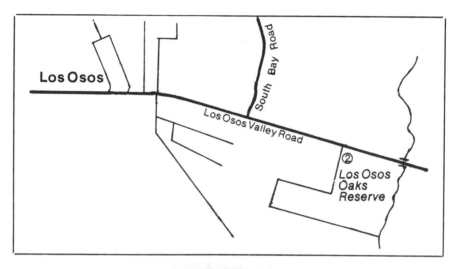

Nature class and teachers perch in the limbs of the big oaks.

The dunes overlook Shark Inlet and Morro Bay.

14—Exploring Morro Bay Sand Spit

When the Clam Taxi took us over to the sand spit across Morro Bay, I had the feeling I was approaching an exotic island in some far distant corner of the globe. The landscape was barren and forlorn, with the debris of the ocean scattered about. It wasn't particularly beautiful; it was strange and austere.

I looked back as the skiff from the Marina Motel pulled away and worked its way back along the buoys and markers. A last goodbye wave and we were on our own. We had parked a second car 3.5 miles south where the spit joins the mainland. It was two p.m. and I wondered if I had allowed enough time to complete the hike. There was only one way to go, now that the boat was gone.

Much of what we were walking across—on the end of the spit to the ocean side—is dredging soil: silty, hard-packed salty stuff, quite different from the natural, wind-blown moving dunes farther south.

We came to the breakwater, a long rib of boulders that forms the south rim of the mouth of the bay. Winter deposits of sand against the south side of the breakwater create great waves and three surfers were out there getting good rides.

The spit is a long finger of moving dunes that encases the bay. When Portola came through here in 1769, the spit did not extend as far north as it does now and Morro Rock stood prominently in the water, "... separated from the coast by a little less than a gunshot." Northwest winds blew in fiercely through an open channel on the rock's north side and on the south side a shallow channel opened and closed with changing seasons and tides.

The WPA in the '30s, and the Army Corps of Engineers in the '40s, changed all that. They extended Atascadero State Beach closing off the mouth of the bay north of Morro Rock. Dredging materials were added to the beach as well as to the spit, bringing the two together until only a narrow navigational channel exists on the south side of Morro Rock.

As we turned southward along the coast, the dunes began to build until soon we had mountains of land to our left and crashing breakers to our right.

Off in the distance two lonely figures moved in the mist, the only other humanoids in this solitary windswept place.

The spit is marvelously desolate. Few people find the inclination to walk its 3.5 mile length, saving it for the rest of us who cherish a wild, primal world of sea and sand.

There are seven posted half-mile markers on the ocean side of the spit. Number one is near the parking lot at the end of the old army road—where the spit joins the mainland—and #7 is at the end of the spit, opposite the town of Morro Bay.

Whales can be seen on their migration from Alaska to Baja California as they pass from Point Estero, north of Cayucos, to Point Buchon, just south of the spit. They are seen southbound from December to January, and returning in February through April.

At marker #6 we observed four vultures recycling a dead seal that washed ashore. Farther along, we kicked up some *pizma*, or *malak*, Indian words for oil blobs that naturally seep from offshore sea floor sources.

There's a good-sized midden at marker #5, a picnic spot where Indians ate large pismo clams and other shellfish harvested from the bay. These shell mounds are so extensive they serve as markers to fishermen at sea. Another shell mound north of marker #1 is over 40 feet deep and may have been used by Indians for over two thousand years. Obsidian and chert fragments suggest that mountain and valley Indians came to the spit for summer vacations, trading tools for seafood. The first fish and chips business catering to tourists was probably established out on the spit long before America was "discovered." The middens are valuable keys to an archaelogical past that should not be disturbed.

As we walked the spit I recalled the stories of the war years when fears of a Japanese invasion on these sandy beaches were real enough to cause defense construction and mock landings. But views of surf fishermen casting lines into the foaming water brought back the peaceful reality of the place. Nothing to worry about today; in fact, this is where worries seem to disappear.

It takes about 1½-2 hours to walk the entire length of the spit, but by taking the Clam Taxi shuttle to the #7 marker across the bay, we were able to walk one way to pick up a second car parked near marker #1. We discovered this system works best if you carry the keys to the second car.

We trudged over the dune to the little Toyota sitting at the end of the old army road, and there was a lot of frantic body slapping and searching as we sought in vain to come up with the keys to the car. The chill winds of evening bit our cheeks as a friendly sun sank beyond the horizon.

A rusty coat hanger was no match for a car that was behaving like a sardine can, and only our most pathetic looks and feeble murmurings saved us from having to walk the 7.5 miles of paved road back to the first car parked at the Marina Motel. A jogger and his dog trotted by and soon returned in his truck to take us back to Morro Bay.

If you plan to use two cars, park one at the end of the old army road, a rutted but passable sand (dirt) road off Pecho Road in Los Osos, about a half mile south of Monarch Lane. (In the summer the sand is soft and the risk of getting stuck is greater than fall and winter.)

Drive the other car to Morro Bay along Los Osos Valley Road to South Bay Boulevard to the Embarcadero. At the Exxon sign is the Morro Bay Marina, at 699 Embarcadero. They've been running people over to the spit for 30 years with their skiff called the Clam Taxi. It runs during the summer months from 9 a.m.–4:30 p.m., and they charge $3 per person for a round trip. Phone 772-8085 for details.

If you don't have a second car at the south end of the spit, the skiff will pick you up whenever you wave them back over.

Another pleasant approach to the spit is to take Los Osos Valley Road through town to Monarch Lane, right to Del Norte, right on Howard, around the Sea Pines Golf Course on Butte and left to Nevada. Park at the dead-end and walk the road along the edge of the bay beside the eucalyptus row until you reach the spit and a vehicle pull off on the right. The large dune at this point has a couple transverse trails along its slope to the top. From there it's downhill to the ocean through one of the great shell mounds.

Better dress for three seasons when you go out there; and take a little water and some snacks. Above all, stuff a wire clothes hanger in your pack. There's always a few of us who depend on people like you.

The old Spooner Ranch house (1892) overlooks the cove at Montana de Oro.

15—Valencia Peak—
Hike Through Geologic History

I was on the edge of the sea, racing at awesome speed toward San Francisco. The fierce wind brought tears to my eyes as I watched foaming breakers throw themselves against the headlands. There I was among old whale bones, fossil shells and millions of tons of diatomacous earth —all taking a ride toward the city with the bay... at about an inch a year.

I wasn't alone. The old Spooner ranch house was coming with me; in fact, the whole set of Montana de Oro State Park was moving. Not only were we moving northward. We were also moving up.

At least that's the theory. And one of the world's largest open air museums at Montana de Oro exhibits this phenomenon. Valencia Peak is just a honey of a mountain to tell the story of the birth and development of our coast. It goes like this:

We're moving on a plate of geography (Pacific Plate) that has risen from the sea, and is moving against another plate (North American Plate). The friction surface is the San Andreas Fault.

Proof that the land is rising from the sea can be seen in the layers that make up Valencia Peak. At 700 feet there is a beach of soft sand. At higher elevations, even at the top (1345 feet), there are marine shells and beach pebbles. Most of the layers are Monterey shale, an organic rock made of compressed layers of microscopic marine diatoms. It obligingly fractures into layers that reveal the secrets of who has lived here.

As you hike the trail to Valencia Peak along numerous switchbacks, you walk back through time over four terraces of old beach. It's only a 1½ hour, two-mile trek up there over a fairly strenuous trail, but the sights are breathtaking.

Take Los Osos Valley Road until it becomes Pecho Road, an old dunes road of the 1930 s that was made when the eucalyptus groves were planted. At the clearing you will see Spooner's Cove on the right and the old Spooner ranch house on the left. Park the family chariot next to the house and go inside for a bit of human history and a visit with the ghosts of the Spooners.

The original A. B. Spooner came to these parts in 1867 as a Methodist circuit rider and part-time boat pilot. He drowned in 1877 when his boat capsized in the turbulent surf. His son, Alden B. Spooner, survived him and eventually owned 8000 acres and six miles of ocean frontage. In 1892 the ranch house was built, with later additions in 1914. The seaside terrace was planted to hay and shipped to the city horses of San Francisco. In 1915 automobiles and streetcars became popular and the hay market weakened. Then dairy cows grazed the hay fields, and a reservoir behind the campground provided water power to run the separators to make butter.

Following the dairy period the seaside bluffs were used to raise produce. This is still being done on the terraces south of the park near Diablo Canyon nuclear plant.

The trail head to the peak begins with a walk from Spooner's ranch house onto Pecho Road, south for 200 yards. On the left the trail ascends through brushy chaparral of sage and yellow monkey flower. After a few hundred yards you gain a good vantage point to observe the seaside bluffs awash in pastel lavender (wild radish) and yellow (mustard) in the spring and summer. This terrace has the numerous seacliff walks. Pick up that trail 250 yards past the ranch house on the right side of the road.

As you continue on the Valencia trail, you rise to the second terrace of Monterey shale. Grasses dominate here and the going is very pleasant.

Climb out of the second terrace through the heavy brush, chockfull of poison oak, to a clearing where other trails branch to the right and left. The left trail can be your alternative return route, which follows an old road back to the ranch house. The trail to the right goes back to Pecho Road.

The main trail ascends sharply from the third terrace. It's a good aerobic trek and in 20 minutes you'll be on top with long expansive views of Hollister Peak, Cayucos and all the canyons in the park. The old Spooner reservoir lies below with splotches of hemlock and thistle growing in the wet seeps.

On the peak you can picnic where hawks and vultures soar. In the summer the marine layer of fog may fill the canyons while Valencia Peak rises into the sunshine. At other times the marine fog covers the peak leaving the lower terraces clear. Be sure to bring binoculars to study the sea traffic and canyon wildlife.

When you are ready an interesting alternative return route is a trail several hundred feet below the peak that drops down toward reservoir flat, to the east and north. You will join the Oats Peak Trail that goes back to the ranch house through the hemlock and thistle patches. Large meadows of golden fiddleneck are in bloom down there, with goldfinches in near swarm numbers flitting through it. It's quite a spectacle.

Climbing Valencia Peak is a good way to observe our jolting slide northward and to get a perspective on human history against a backdrop of infinite cosmic antiquity.

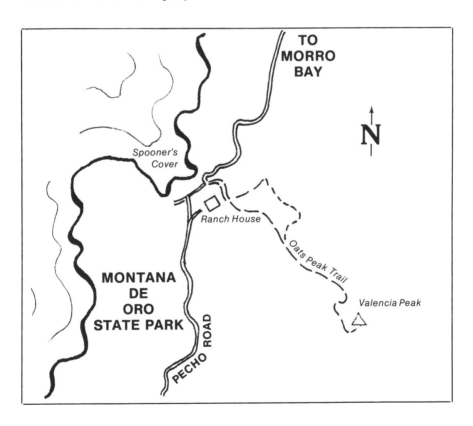

The beautiful Victorian home is now a bed and breakfast inn.

16—Arroyo Grande Bicycle Tour— Bicycle Touring Through The Land of Branch

Around 1780 the mission in San Luis was having trouble growing the food it needed, so it began raising crops in the Arroyo Grande Valley. The valley was broad and thickly covered with monte, a shrubby flood plain community of blackberries, willow and sycamore. When cleared and planted, the land produced extraordinary crops of corn, beans, squash and chili peppers.

A New Yorker by the name of Francis Ziba Branch came into the valley in 1833 while on an otter-hunting expedition from Santa Barbara. He looked enviously at the fertile land and vowed he would someday own this valley. In three years he was back to make good on his claim, and eventually to establish the village of Arroyo Grande.

Conveniently Branch married Dona Manuela Carlona, who was of mixed Spanish and Aztec ancestry. Branch's marriage entitled him to file claim for a Mexican land grant and in 1836 Branch moved onto his new 17,000-acre Santa Manuela Rancho with his wife and newborn son. When Manuela saw the Arroyo Grande Valley from the top of a hill for the first time, Francis Branch called out to her, "Look, Manuela. All that you see is ours!" She looked . . . and cried. She saw nothing but wilderness, loneliness and hardship. For years their only companions were the Indians who occupied Corralitos Canyon after they were forced to leave the mission in 1833. But she stuck by her darling for 39 years and long outlived him, dying in 1909 at the age of 94.

For this 15-mile bicycle tour take Route 101 to Halcyon Road, the first Arroyo Grande exit. At the bottom of the ramp and to your right is the old Odd Fellows Cemetery, donated by a man in 1883 who was kicked by a horse and became its first resident.

One block west along Halcyon is the Methodist Church where you can park your car while you put your bicycle on the road. Go south on Halcyon one mile to the town of Halcyon.

The Halcyon Community is a philosophical, religious and humanitarian society whose founders arrived in 1904 from New York to live in peace, work and serve their fellowmen. From 1904–1930 the Halcyonites operated the Coffee-Rice Mansion on Route 1 in Oceano as a sanitarium for the treatment of tuberculosis, nervous disorders and alcoholism.

The Temple of the People, seen from Halcyon Road, is the center of the lives of the people who live in the 20 Temple homes. It teaches the brotherhood of man and the Karmic responsibility of man to his world.

Turn right on Temple Street for a closer look at the 1923 Temple and think about attending their daily noon meeting or their 10:30 a.m. Sunday service. The University Center and Hiawatha Lodge next door, were the centers for Arroyo Grande's cultural life during the '30s.

Ride through the six streets of charmingly rustic frame homes ensconced under the towering canopies of 80-year-old trees. The house at 1480 Dower Street, named after Dr. Dower, an early founder, operated as a tuberculosis sanitarium. On your way out on La Due Street, stop at the Halcyon Store on Halcyon Road. It carries health food, junk food, wood chimes, sun bonnets, embroidered pillows . . . and is the community's post office.

Turn right on Halcyon to Route 1, left to Valley Road and left .5 mile to the Rose Victorian Inn, formerly the Pitkin residence, built in 1885. The Pitkin House, and the Coffee-Rice Mansion on Route 1 in Oceano, were built at the same time, by the same builder.

The country inn is beautifully restored and serves dinners Thursday–Sunday, and Sunday brunch. The gazebo and garden are popular for alfresco concerts, parties and weddings. Inn tours are possible when guests are not in residence.

Back to your bicycles (or car) ride north to Fair Oaks Avenue. Stop at the high school for a look at Branch's millstone that serves as a base for the flagpole. The flour mill operated near the Branch home along Branch Mill Road until 1894.

From the high school go northeast to Traffic Way, right two blocks to East Cherry Avenue, then left. A quarter mile east on Cherry is Pacific Coast Railway Place, where the narrow gauge (three feet from rail to rail) railway chugged into town from the Santa Ynez Valley. It ran from 1882-1940 bringing chickens, pigs and produce to San Luis Obispo.

In a half mile Cherry Avenue becomes Branch Mill Road which rims the Arroyo Grande Valley, turning northerly. In .7 mile Newsom Canyon Road takes off to the right. This is the old stage coach road that ran up to Newsom Springs and over Newsom Ridge to Los Berros Road and the Rancho Nipomo of Captain William Dana. The horses always complained about this incline up Newsom Canyon and you probably will too.

It's a mile up to the Newsom Spring Resort that functioned from 1870–90. It was the hub of social activity for prominent families who had summer cottages there. The music and laughter are gone, and the last cottages were destroyed in 1985. In 1991 the last half-mile of Newsom Spring Road was gated, so you'll have to turn around and simply imagine life from the past. Water still issues from the ground—40 gallons a minute at 100.1 degrees but its use is now strictly for the ranchers who own the land.

Continue north on Branch Mill Road and enjoy the pastoral scenes of cabbage and pepper fields. Around 1900 a 57.5 pound cabbage was grown here. By 1908 there was a race track below the quaint houses, where free-for-all harness races drew large crowds and the town band entertained everyone with rousing marches and polkas.

In 1.4 miles Branch Mill approaches Huasna Road, then continues north .8 mile to the original Branch homestead, .1 mile south of School Road. There's a large mound of earth on the left side of the road and an old gray shack with a willow growing over it. The original two-story new England style adobe house has melted back into the ground, leaving a large mound. The Branch mill operated near here until 1894, using water from Arroyo Grande Creek.

A mile north is the old Branch Mill School, a single-gabled cracker box (building) overlooking the Arroyo Grande Valley, nearly at the end of Cecchetti Road. Turn left on Cecchetti to Lopez Drive, then left again to Arroyo Grande. Jog left on Branch Street and come through this village of 19th century frame homes and store fronts.

As you leave the old town along Branch, it will become Grand Avenue beyond Highway 101. At Halcyon turn right to the Methodist Church, completing the leisurely 15-mile loop in about three or four hours.

Swimming holes in the Lopez Wilderness canyons.

17—The Wet, Rocky Road to Big and Little Falls

The paved road became dirt just beyond the conference grounds behind Lopez Reservoir. In a moment I was sitting in front of a creek that was running right through the road.

The creek was 20-feet wide and the water was running at a pretty good clip. It didn't look like an invitation for my new compact car.

From out of the woods ahead a pickup rambled into view and without hesitation rolled into the stream, bouncing around on the stream boulders.

Dripping like a long-haired dog the truck pulled alongside. A moustached face leaned out the window: "You gonna try to make it through in that thing?" I did not take this as encouragement.

"No," I said to myself, "I'm not going to waste my car doing creek crossings to see some falls and canyon pools that probably aren't worth seeing anyway." I grabbed the gear shift and stuck it in reserve.

But a small voice muttered, "Nothing ventured—nothing gained."

I shifted into low and drove into the creek. The front end squirmed around on the slippery boulders while water lapped against the doors. I cursed myself for foolish ventures.

The compact cakewalked through the stream and gingerly gripped the rising road. This was fun!

Creek crossing number two came before my grin disappeared. My worried frown returned.

I entered the water for the second time. Little 13-inch wheels felt their way along the bottom, stumbling over rocks and chasing newts. Made it easy.

Only 12 more creek crossings to go.

I had to stop for a moment to see where I was. This riparian habitat behind Lopez Lake is very different from the chaparral on top. The California bay leaves and maples love to grow here. Maiden-hair, woodwardia and sword ferns grip the canyon walls, and miner's lettuce is abundant.

At the fifth creek I passed by a couple who had pulled upstream in their jeep to picnic. Water ran beneath their folding chairs as they sipped a cool one and waved. The place is so idyllic I nearly forgot it was the falls I had come to see.

After the seventh creek and 1.5 miles from the Lopez Canyon Conference Grounds, the road broadens. A sign on the right marks the trail to Little Falls. The trail goes by an old metal building whose slab sides bear the perverse messages of generations of nature lovers. I didn't look —much.

There are a number of water-carved wading pools along the half-mile walk to the falls, but the niftiest pools are up above. Near the falls a path ascends sharply up on the right side. There in the shade of the maples and bay trees are a number of romantic, naturally-sculpted tubs, just right for soaking, lounging and lunching on a hot summer day.

I returned to my car to continue my spring spawning run up the creek. At 2.7 miles the road becomes the creek for at least 700 feet. It wasn't too bad, but in wet weather I know it's a terror.

At 3.8 miles I saw a small falls on the left and a number of vans and pickups parked about helter-skelter. Big Falls is a half-mile hike up the canyon to the right. The layout is like that of Little Falls, with a trail on the right going up very steeply to the pools and grottoes above.

A rope hangs from a tree above the first pool, inviting swingers to take off for a plunge into water so deep jumpers from the 50-foot cliffs above never touch bottom.

If you stay on the Big Falls Canyon trail, you will pass another falls in a mile. At the top of the Ridge, a mile and a half beyond the second falls, you can look over the Salinas River drainage and Lake Santa Margarita, only six miles away. The trail loops back toward the Little Falls Canyon along the High Mountain Road, a total distance of about five miles.

When you go to the falls, arrive before noon and leave while the sun is still high in the sky. You don't want to be the last one out in case of emergencies and mishaps.

What kind of vehicle should you use? Four-wheel drives are best, trucks and vans are good and sedans can make it if you have an appetite for adventure and uncertainty. This is a good time to tune up your mother-in-law's Impala and take a test drive up the creeks. We packed eight people in a Buick station wagon once. We made it; but if you see a Buick tail pipe out there anywhere, let me know. We're missing one.

A friend and I tried it on a motorcycle. Two people on two wheels crossing a stream with algae-covered rocks is similar to snorkeling on a motorcycle.

You can also bicycle in from the conference grounds. Mountain bikes are best. Or hike in. It's only 1.5 miles to Little Falls. Either way be prepared to get wet.

Not ready for any of this? Then at least take the seven mile drive in from Lake Lopez on blacktop to the Lopez Canyon Conference Grounds. At the entrance to Lopez Lake Recreation Area, High Mountain Road to Pozo turns right paralleling an extension of Lopez Lake. In one mile Upper Lopez Canyon Road goes left to Little and Big Falls, past Camp French (Boys Scouts Of America) and the conference grounds.

The blue ceanothus (California lilac) in the chaparral is stunning in spring, and the canyon sunflower and prickly phlox are showy along the roadside. The views of expansive valleys and rugged wilderness are among the best on the coast.

The hills back of Lopez Lake are part of Los Padres National Forest and contiguous with the Santa Lucia Wilderness Area. The fossils of scallops and sand dollars suggest this was the edge of the sea millions of years ago. The stratified rock is easily broken and has no particular use —except to beautify our world and hold our water in secret until we need it.

We rode over rolling dunes and among old Indian campsites.

18—Horseback Riding The Beaches And Back Dunes of Oceano

It doesn't seem so long ago since my high school friends and I raced horses along level Illinois bridle paths. The trails wound through groves of oak trees and open fields. Hell bent for leather we galloped under hanging limbs and pounded trails better suited for meditative walks.

I'm a little older and wiser now. The horse has a kinder rider but when Dan, at the Livery Stables in Oceano, reminded me that my horse may lie down in the stream if I let him, I firmed up my grip and sat heavy in the saddle to give the horse the impression I was in charge.

"You don't mean this horse is going to lie down in the stream with me on him?" I asked.

"Yes, but don't let him. Keep him moving when you get in the middle of the creek. Most horses will want to lie down in the water on a warm day."

How tender, I thought, horse and rider lying down together, in the middle of a cold stream.

Before we mounted our steeds we read the waiver: ". . . waive liability for horses that might bite, kick, lie down, go swimming, bolt, buck, run, stop suddenly, rear or otherwise misbehave."

Fair enough. Bring on our horses.

The Oceano stables (Livery Stables, Inc.) is a long-established and reliable stable located in the bok choy and cabbage fields off 22nd Street behind the Oceano Dunes.

The atmosphere at the stable is a happy barnyard mix of dogs and horses with the aromatic ambience of manure and sweaty leather. Dusty cowboys with a kinship to horses walk in the corral selecting horses for particular riders. First skittish, then passive, the horses are led to the hitching posts while the repetitive task of attaching 40 pounds of saddle is completed. A feed bag of horse M&M's is hung on the horse's head while the tack is adjusted.

With the horse mellowed out it is moved over to a three-step staircase where the rider mounts—about as easily as mounting a bar stool. No throwing your body over the horse as in old Ronald Reagan films. The stable caters to the novice rider, some consolation if you haven't been on a horse lately—or ever. Livery Stables, Inc. assured me they have a horse suited for every rider.

"Nevada. Reno Nevada. When you ride him, you gamble," said Dan good naturedly as he introduced me to my steed for the day. He's good looking enough to make *Sunset Magazine* but was no gamble at all. I thought he was a one-way horse that showed some spirit only when his nose pointed toward the stable. When I returned, Dan mounted this seemingly lethargic gelding and turned him into a snorting stallion that danced like he was on hot coals. Nevada had pegged me as an old softy. He had manipulated me and exploited me for my kindness. I felt used. My daughter rode Christy, a rambunctious brown mare who loved to run. With the grin of a kid on Christmas morning, Cynthia flew with Christy, a beautiful tangle of blond and brown hair racing along the beach.

The trail from the stable follows the Arroyo Grande Creek along a man-made levee. In dark water streaming with graceful strands of green algae, a snowy egret stood in total concentration, with visions of minnows and crayfish dancing in its wee little head. Nearby two ducks, upended, scoured the creek for worms and snails.

A rustic country house along the trail, ensconced in piney woods and ringed with black poplar and willow, seems a long way from the blowouts and the slipfaced dunes on the ocean front, but is actually only a few hundred yards.

From there our horses carried us to the secondary dunes. Beach grass, ice plant, verbena and dune buckwheat grip the restless sandy knolls and make them ecstatically colorful. We were lost in reverie as we rode through rolling hillocks and among old Indian campsites where bleached shells cover the ground. No need to worry about getting really lost. Slacken the reins and nudge your horse and you'll be heading back toward the stables in the amount of time it takes a horse to think of oats.

We found that it's best to walk the horses through these secondary dunes before you get to the beach on the main trail. After they've been to the beach and are headed back, it takes a strong hand to turn their heads back into the dunes.

The trail to the beach goes through a grove of willow and poplar, then opens out onto the beach, with the creek running across the path. Look for a shallow spot and steer your horse across it. Remember, you're the driver; don't let him stop midstream and lie down.

Many of the horses are used to being kicked out when they get to the beach and experienced riders relish the exhilaration of running on the beach. There are 15 miles of open beach for you to ride on, but Livery Stables, Inc. limits your riding time on any one horse to three hours.

I can't think of a better way to experience our coastal dunes than on a well-behaved horse. Creaking leather and 800 pounds of undulating horse flesh sets loose the mind yearning to escape into a world of sweet smells and sights. You will see things witnessed by few mortals and your spirit will be as refreshed as a horse galloping through the surf.

Where, What and How Much.

Take Route 1 through Oceano to 22 Street. Turn toward the ocean (west) .2 mile across a bridge and the Amtrak rails to Silver Spur Place, on a dirt farm road, .5 mile to the livery entrance. Call Livery Stables, Inc. at 489-8100 for information.

—Wear tough jeans and boots or shoes with heels.

—The rate is $15/hour, with a $25 cash deposit.

—Hours are 8 a.m.–4 p.m. during the summer.

Livery Stables, Inc. also has overnight boarding and longer term boarding services.

The dunes area north of Mussell Rock to the Pismo Beach State Park and recreational vehicle area boundry is under the central administration of the Nature Conservancy. The coastal lands must be assured of the sanctity befitting a wild area of unexcelled scenic diversity. Access is permitted at Main Street to Guadalupe Beach and at Oso Flaco Lake; day use permits and annual passes are on a fee basis. For information write the Nature Conservancy, P.O. Box 15810, San Luis Obispo, CA 93406 or phone (805) 545-9925.

The trail along the lake is through a canopy of miniature willow and wax myrtle.

19—Coreopsis Hill Hike—
A Dark Green Dune Bright With
Flowers in the Springtime

On Saturday, September 2, 1769, Don Gaspar de Portola led a mile-long line of Spanish soldiers and Indian guides into San Luis Obispo County.

The pack train of 63 men and 180 mules and horses wandered into the dunes near Guadalupe, searching for the uncluttered open beaches. The craggy headlands at Mussel Point had forced them inland through heavy brush.

In the evening they came to a round lake in a swampy area, covered with rushes and grass. Bears were seen and the soldiers succeeded in bagging one for dinner. I imagine that as Portola ate his bear steak that night he muttered, "oso flaco" (skinny bear), a name that marks the place today.

It's also likely that on that evening they ate watercress, which they called *los berros*. Wild gooseberries and strawberries grew in the area and they could have ended their meal with a fruit compote.

Portola and his band continued down the beach toward Pismo and then on through Price Canyon to a valley where they saw seven bears. The Franciscan fathers and Portola concluded that . . . "this is a grand place for a fine mission."

Our group of hikers observed Oso Flaco Lake and the wide variety of waterfowl—teals, cormorants, western and pied-billed grebes and a host of shore birds. This is a great place to sit with a pair of field glasses and a bird book.

Since off-road vehicles have been banned in this area whistling swans have returned and in the evenings coyotes can be seen.

We followed the trail along the lake toward the ocean and over some dunes. The trail soon enters a stand of willow and wax myrtle so dense a tunnel has been cut through. With only dancing flickers of light hitting the trail, we walked like creatures in Lilliput under a canopy of minature trees.

The trail follows the arroyo that drains the lake to the ocean. I know you've been to the ocean a thousand times but this approach is a surprise. From here to the Santa Maria River is a wilderness area that has been designated by the U.S. Fish and Wildlife Service as the most pristine natural area in the state of California.

One of our party picked up a glob of tar-oil on the beach. Technological garbage, right? Wrong. These globs have been surfacing and washing ashore for thousands of years. The Chumash Indians called it *pizmu*, and the beach where they frequently found it . . . Pizmu Beach, of course. The Indians used the pitch to seal their plank boats and woven baskets.

Most of the hikers removed their shoes to cross the creek on our way to Coreopsis Hill. Some of us who tried vaulting it ended up in the middle.

Cutting eastward sharply beyond the creek we made our way across a quarter mile of open dune. We spotted an illegal cache of clam shells on the left as we trudged through landscape as lonely as the surface of the moon.

Coreopsis Hill is a dark green dune straight ahead. It's well-covered with a healthy growth of vegetation and stands out conspicuously from the surrounding dunes. There is a path up its western face but it's best to walk on the vegetation to reduce erosion. The plants are well rooted and can take occasional human trampling; it's motorized vehicles that do the damage.

The Giant Coreopsis grows here, sometimes to five feet or more. The feathery green foliage grows on a stem the color and texture of an elephant's trunk. The bright yellow flowers resemble brown-eyed Susans. Their big kick is the first weeks of March. The prickly phlox, wild strawberry and bush lupine then take their turns to bloom.

A good place to have lunch is down the hill by the black poplar grove, alongside Little Oso Flaco Lake.

You have two ways to get back to your car. Go back the way you came in or continue walking the trail eastward on the slope of Coreopsis Hill facing the produce fields, until you reach a farm road. Take this left to the paved road, another left and you're a quarter mile from your car. Total trip is about two miles.

To get to Oso Flaco Lake and Coreopsis Hill, follow Highway 1 southward across those 15,000-year-old dunes, the Nipomo Mesa, until you leave the eucalyptus groves. You will descend into a broad valley of cabbage, sprouts and celery. Take the first road to your right (Oso Flaco Road) until it dead ends at Oso Flaco Lake.

The Oso Flaco wetlands, creek and beach area are one of the Central Coast's largest refuges for migrating shorebirds as well as habitat for the endangered least tern. A concerted program is underway to protect the fragile habitat and to ensure the survival of the many rare and endangered species that reside here. Boardwalks to the sea protect the valuable natural resources and provide the visitor easy access to the variety of dune habitats.

The dunes area north of Mussell Rock to the Pismo Beach State Park and recreational vehicle area boundry is under the central administration of the Nature Conservancy. The coastal lands must be assured of the sanctity befitting a wild area of unexcelled scenic diversity. Access is permitted at Main Street to Guadalupe Beach and at Oso Flaco Lake; day use permits and annual passes are on a fee basis. For information write the Nature Conservancy, P. O. Box 15810, San Luis Obispo, CA 93406 or phone (805) 545-9925.

Osos Flaco Lake and creek are in the heart of the proposed national seashore.

Old Route 46 is ideal for rides in the country.

Santa Rita Old Creek Road is a seldom used line between Templeton and Cayucos.

20—Motorcyling the Back Roads From Pismo Beach to Cambria

Don't think motorcycling is for the young only. Young at heart, yes, but when I met Ruth Gabriel recently, and learned of her group of senior friends, the Heaven's Angels, and their travels around the county on their motorcycles, I knew that one of my pet stereotypes was in for a beating.

Just about everyone has had experience driving or riding on a motorcycle. For most of us the encounter comes early in life, about the time we had our first love and when we sold our bicycle for a guitar. Our interest in riding may have lasted as long as it takes to acquire raspberry burns from a fall on pavement.

For others of us the exhiliration of streaking through space astride 50 horsepower, smashing insects on our teeth and having tears in our ears is too good to ever give up.

We savor those moments cruising down country roads on a warm summer day, smelling new mown hay and the bouquets of wild fragrances spread out like invisible plumes. People in cars never sense these great moments in the life of a nose. Bicyclists are usually gasping and suffering so much they neither see nor smell. Only motorcyclists know what it's like to ride in relative leisure and comfort, plowing through hordes of mating gnats or riding in the rain when droplets hit like gun shot.

For Ruth and her friends, for all middle-age bikers who have never grown up, and for all younger bikers who unabashedly revel in the exuberance of riding—I've got a ride for you.

South county riders begin your motorcycle day trip in Pismo Beach on Route 1, and go north through Shell Beach on Shell Beach Road past Spyglass, until you come to Avila Road. Turn left and go to Avila Hot Springs. Stop in for a swim or massage, or a coffee break under the palm trees. Turn right on San Luis Bay Drive to See Canyon Road for a ride up See Canyon and over the Irish Hills. You'll catch incredibly beautiful views of the Irish Hills and the Los Osos Valley, with the Nine Sisters (Morros) all lined up forming the north wall of the valley.

As you come down from the top the road will intersect with Los Osos Valley Road, where you'll meet the San Luis riders coming out of the city. (See Canyon Road becomes Prefumo Canyon Road on the north side.)

Turn left on Los Osos Valley Road and ride beyond Foothill Drive to Turri Road, halfway toward Los Osos. This road is a gem with lots of curves and dog legs. Hollister Peak comes down to the roadside allowing intimate viewing of this granite mass as you drive toward South Bay Boulevard. Turn right and pass the mud flats of Morro Bay. Stop here and set up your folding lawn chairs for an hour of bird watching. This is Audubon country and one of the richest areas in the world for open water, shoreline and woodland fowl. You might also want to unpack the easel and palette for a little painting.

Continue your ride by taking a sharp left on Country Club Drive toward Morro Bay alongside the Morro Bay Golf Course, where you can warm up the old clubs on a course called Poor Man's Pebble Beach. Country Club Drive becomes Main Street Morro Bay and then joins Route 1, running north toward Cayucos.

Cayucos is as quaint as an old attic chest, and full of antiques and collectibles. You probably won't have room for more than a small dresser and a few lamps, but after shopping look for Montecito Road off Route 1, on the south end of town. This becomes Cypress Mountain Road and will take you into the back country, away from the ocean. As you climb you'll pass Cow Camp and Whale Rock Reservoir, water supply for the California Men's Colony, Cal Poly University and San Luis Obispo.

You can't swim in the reservoir, but fish can, and trout are biting— sometimes. Unlatch your minnow bucket, rod and reel and that irreplaceable tackle box for an afternoon of exciting angling. There are a few posted do's and don'ts. The important are: "*Do* keep your dog on a leash," and "*Don't* throw your cold coffee in the reservoir."

Going along Cypress Mountain Road you'll travel through a picturesque riparian habitat, still gurgling, and shaded by maples and sycamores. These streams offer some fascinating rocks for your garden. You might want to tie a few on.

The road leaves the stream side and skirts grassy knolls and fields of hay bales. It's a narrow macadam road in good repair and curly enough to dissuade people who want to make time. This road is for the easy rider who couldn't care less where the road is going.

Cypress Mountain Road crosses Route 46, built in 1974, and the name changes to Santa Rosa Creek road. This is actually old Route 46 to Cambria and has been in use since around 1860 when it sufficed as a dirt trail from Cambria to Paso Robles. It was impassable in the winter for many years and was dangerously narrow and steep until the state oiled it in 1939 and later paved it.

For 18 miles, past ridges of pine and ribbons of cut hay in stubbly fields, you gain views of the ocean to the west; then the road winds down close to streams where orchards and berry fields beautify the land. At Linn's Fruit Bin, four miles from Cambria, it's time to get off your bike again for some berry picking. The olallie berries are just about through but there is good boysenberry picking. John Linn makes some memorable pies, and you may want to pick up a raspberry-rhubard pie for dessert. You can eat it there or you can take it to Shamel Park in town for a picnic.

We had a good lunch in old town Cambria (east village) at Picnique In The Pines restaurant. They have a grazing menu that allows you to take small samples of a lot of creatively prepared foods. If you buy a picnic basket from Banbury Cross (or bring your own), Picnique will pack it with croissants, pates, salads, scones and other sinful delectables. Head for the ocean on Windsor Boulevard to Shamel Park where you can cook out or spread your picnic basket goodies on the lawn. A good place to use the badminton set you lugged along, too.

For an alternative return route, take Route 1 from Cambria back to Cayucos and get on Cypress Mountain Road (Montecito) again. At the top of Whale Rock Reservoir, Santa Rita Old Creek Road takes off from the right. For a mile it's paved, then becomes dirt and stays rutted, dusty and pocked for the next ten miles while it runs through some *very* rugged country, rimming jagged peaks with precipitous canyons below. I was amazed how close wilderness is within our easy grasp. Fifteen miles from Cayucos Santa Rita Road comes into Vineyard Road in Templeton. From there Route 101 will take you back home.

Come to think of it, this trip is O.K. for automobile travelers as well. And if you're in your car and you see a motorcyclist looking like he's got everything imaginable strapped to himself and his bike, blow your horn and wave. He may wave back—if he can.

The Whale Rock Reservoir is open 6 a.m.–7 p.m. for trout fishing from the last Saturday of April until November 15, Wednesday–Sunday, and all legal holidays. Call 995-3701 for information.

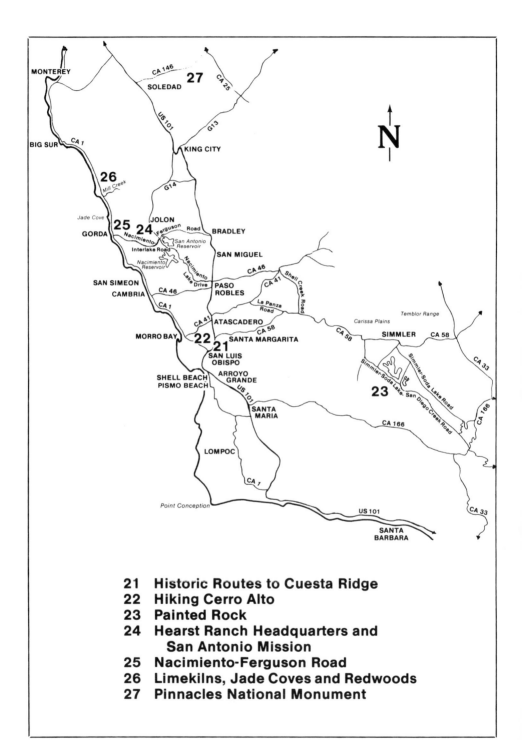

21 **Historic Routes to Cuesta Ridge**
22 **Hiking Cerro Alto**
23 **Painted Rock**
24 **Hearst Ranch Headquarters and San Antonio Mission**
25 **Nacimiento-Ferguson Road**
26 **Limekilns, Jade Coves and Redwoods**
27 **Pinnacles National Monument**

III Points North

The 1873 stage coach trail wanders to the top of Cuesta Grade.

21—Historic Routes to Cuesta Ridge

I've got a wonderful Sunday afternoon drive for you, Kathleen. I know you haven't been getting out much since you broke your hip, so get Gaylord to warm up the Pinto for a ride in the country along the traveled way. There's some beautiful fall color and I'll throw in a little history for your amusement.

The traveled way is what they used to call the old Padre Trail and Stage Coach Road going out of San Luis Obispo towards the Cuesta Grade. It probably won't be as new to you as it was to me. I thought I had made another great discovery until I talked to Pherbe and Harold and some other old timers. Pherbe said, "Oh yeah, it's been there for a long time." Then proceeded to fill me with stories and details.

Now if you can get Gaylord to drive you off the mesa to the outskirts of San Luis on Monterey Street I'll begin your tour at the Motel Inn, some say the first roadside stopover in the nation to coin the word "motel." Stop here and set your trip odometer at 0.0

The old state highway went right in front of the Motel Inn in 1927 when the motel was built. The old road runs north, then veers left under the present highway alongside the Last Chance Saloon, now part of the Cuesta Park Animal Hospital that's in Cuesta Park.

O.K., Gaylord, drive on to Route 101 going north and in a half mile (.5) pull off on the right side, on Fox Hollow Road. This is the old country road that predates the state highway of 1911. It circles past the ranch house down there and parallels the creek back toward town.

The early dirt county road came by the city reservoir which is at the bend of Fox Hollow Road, next to the creek. It hasn't been used for years and is empty now. From 101 it looks like a large, low corrugated metal building. To the other side (west) of 101 is another reservoir built in 1912.

Back on the road, Gaylord, until you spot a group of palm trees on the right side (1.3 miles). This is Estrada Gardens, named after the Joaquin Estrada family, grantees of the fabulous Santa Margarita Ranch. The Estradas came upon hard times and, in exchange for their vast holdings north of the grade, came here and settled on 160 acres. Herman Mehlmann improved this land after he bought it and planted magnolias, an apricot orchard and many palm trees. A dance pavilion and barbecue area made it the center of SLO social life until shortly after the war when it fell into disuse and neglect. For years the Estrada adobe stood here, visible from the road, a landmark along the traveled way.

You won't be able to jump the gate and walk the gardens, Kathleen, but let me tell you that the memories of warm summer evenings, when laughter and music filled the air, are still there. The barbecue pits along the creek are black and sooty and the creek looks like the kind couples and kids love. The apricot trees that Harold Miossi use to pick when he was a kid are hanging on to life by a thread and the palms are feeling the stress of neglect. It's a sad scene. Cows graze unknowingly along memory lanes. How I wish these relics of the past could be preserved as a county or city park.

At 2.5 miles on the left is the Nevada House, 1895, built at the time of the completion of the Southern Pacific Railroad by a family from Nevada. It's a smashing three-story red and white Victorian that serves as a welcome to everybody coming down the grade. By the United Farm Real Estate office across the road at 2.6 miles is the site of the 1846 Fremont Camp. Captain John C. Fremont "stormed" into town one early morning and "took" San Luis for the U.S. Nobody in town remembered seeing him, hearing him or much less cared what he was up to; but Fremont logged it as a victory.

At 3.4 miles a loop of old highway is seen on the left and up a short way at 3.6 is a pull off near a large billboard. Stop here.

You can hike from here up to the 1922 road above the sign. You can't see the pavement until you're up there, but there it is, a ribbon of narrow concrete with high scuffed curbs, looping in and out of the canyons. Huge bay and sycamore trees hang pendulously over the road now, adding organic debris to the surface so the concrete can hardly be seen. The old Greyhound busses to San Francisco used to brush each other on these narrow roads.

Look over to the west side and you can see the railroad grade at about the same elevation as the highway. The 1873 stage coach trail is over on that side too. You may be able to see it as it meanders through the trees. There was a rash of stagecoach holdups in the 1860s and '70s because of the extensive cover for bandits.

As you continue driving north on 101, remnants of old highway are strewn about like elbow macaroni, sometimes above the present road and sometimes below. At 5.2 miles from the Motel Inn, you will crest the summit (elevation 1522). From here the land slopes northward, forming the Salinas River drainage and the Salinas Valley. Steinbeck's Salinas is downhill 120 miles away at 80 feet above sea level. Keep going north on 101, but get in the left lane for a left turn in a couple of miles.

The railroad's longest tunnel passes underneath the summit and, by the time you see it again, it's on your right side.

At 6.5 miles—eight miles from the San Luis Mission—is the historic Eight Mile House, across from the Southern Pacific Railroad and the Santa Margarita Creek. In 1877 it was along the gravel county road and served as a livery and hotel. The lively arts flourished here in the large octangonal dance pavilion. The house is buried in trees and can be seen better as you turn back south at the next left turn.

Coming up at 6.9 miles is a sign that says "Santa Margarita Exit, One Mile" and a turn off on the left to Tassajara Canyon. Make a U turn here and go back south on 101. Watch the oncoming south traffic or you'll have a Peterbilt in your trunk.

Stay to your right at 8.0 miles because there is a little, obscure road that squirts off to the right side just before the guard rail. Take it. It makes a dip and there you are on the 1927 summit grade road of yesteryear. The railroad and 101 are on your left. There's some pretty color up here, Kathleen. The toyon berries are crimson, the sycamores yellow and the poison oak is as red as Christmas ribbon.

At 8.5 miles you pass Cuesta Glenn, a 1917 roadside waystation, decorated with objects d'art and elk antlers.

At 8.7 you'll rejoin 101. Stay to your right, pass through the truck parking area and make a sharp right onto a paved road that becomes the Cuesta Ridge Road. The old Stage Coach Trail is at this juncture, going left (south and down) towards the city.

The Cuesta Ridge Road, also commonly called TV Tower Road, traverses the ridge westerly, for about 12 miles, with wonderful vistas over San Luis and the Chorro Valley. It's a great place for soaring hawks and hang-gliding humans who pick up the winds that whip up the slopes.

I joined Lonnie Belden and his Cuesta College class for a walk through the sylvan forest four miles from 101 along the paved road. This is a three-mile wide forest of elfin Sargent cypress, growing in the serpentine rock soil, tolerating the high levels of magnesium that prove to be toxic for many other plants. The cypress are in a marked botanical reserve and are one of the distinctive features of our area, an island of rare trees occupying a unique niche.

Growing in among the Sargent cypress are manzanita, big cone pine and digger pine visible at lower, drier, hotter elevations.

I tried driving the Cuesta Ridge Road to its end but the road gets really rough after 11.5 miles, and even four-wheel-drive vehicles can't make it over the chasm to Route 41 and the Cerro Alto Campground only a short distance away.

Find a good place to turn around, Gaylord, and I'll head you down the Stage Coach Road to town. Reset your odometer.

Where the Cuesta Ridge Road meets 101 is where the gravel Stage Coach Road descends. In 0.3 mile you'll see a large painted rock on the right advertising machine repair and restrooms (19th century billboards). To the left at the clearing you can look down on the 1772 Padre Trail going up the bottom of the canyon, and the 1911, 1920, and 1947 sections of the highway over on the east side.

At 0.5 is a grove of eucalyptus, probably planted around 1880. Off to your right at .6 mile is a spur going up to the railroad grade. It's just a short hike up to the rails for a look at the tunnels.

Along the Stage Coach Road at 1.5 miles is the confluence of the 1772 Padre Trail and the 1873 Stage Coach Trail. A house of the 1880s is at 1.8 miles, then at 2.7 miles you come to the present highway again.

If the Highway Department had its way in 1967, we would have had 80 million tons of earth moved into this valley to form an eight-lane grapevine instead of this tiered history of transportation in the Cuesta Canyon.

One last stop, Gaylord. Drive into town and get off at Monterey, then turn right along Loomis to Cuesta Park. Straight ahead is the Cuesta Park Animal Hospital built onto the Last Chance Saloon, a brothel that did well (or bad) until 1940. The far right side of the building shows the original structure.

Past the yellow and black Union Oil barrier is a glimpse of the 1911 state highway that used to run by the saloon. As grade school kids Harold Miossi and his brother waited for the school bus at the gate to their ranch on the left, playing "Your car, my car." Harold recalls it was sometimes five minutes between cars, then he'd bet on it being "his car" if it sounded like a new one.

Cuesta Park is a nice place to have lunch with Kathleen, Gaylord. I hope you filled the basket with a little wine and some good things to eat.

22—Hiking Cerro Alto—
A Window Seat to the World

It was in the springtime when I first rode up Route 41 from Morro Bay to Atascadero. New calves romped in green pastures and the hills were brushed with the yellow of mustard. Old barns with long sloping roofs were tucked into the hills, making the scene as peaceful and pastoral as any I've seen.

I relived that earlier experience the other day as I drove up from Morro Bay, and again I was struck with the beauty of this land. This time I came to hike Cerro Alto.

Seven miles up from Route 1 I turned into Cerro Alto Campground and drove the long road to the parking area by the ranger's residence.

Before we set off on the hike Mary Coffeen assembled our small group for a look at two beautiful Santa Lucia firs that have been planted on the grounds. They're found in remote back country areas so this was a good opportunity to see an endemic species close at hand.

The trail to Cerro Alto begins across the road from the two big firs, on a foot bridge over Morro Creek. The trail starts climbing away from the running creek immediately, proceeding along a weeping slope where maidenhair ferns grow. In less than a quarter mile we left the oaks and sycamores and were headed into the treeless chaparral.

Along the way we stopped to look at the tiny pink flowers of manzanita and the new flowers of toyon. By December those toyon flowers will produce decorative Christmas berries.

We tramped by a pretty little fern grotto, then came to an open area where wild clematis (virgin's bower) was spreading its beautiful self over the chamise and ceanothus.

Hidden from view the wren tits sounded their introductory chirps and then dropped their ping pong ball, or at least that's what it sounded like. They're one of the principal birds of the shrubby chaparral.

Across a draw we could see a clump of madrone trees, and then soon up on the trail we came to a moist area where a number of fine specimens grew. Their limbs were as round and smooth as a baby's leg, with leaves that resemble magnolia.

Nearby a bed of Indian warrior flourished, a cluster of purple flowers in the center of fern-like leaves. They have a partial parasitic relationship with the woody plants in the neighborhood by tapping into their roots.

We had hiked for about an hour with frequent stops to see the developing spring plants. Far below us the canyon bottom of maples and sycamores still looked winter gray.

At about .8 mile, and an elevation of 1400 feet, we came to the AT&T cable road and firebreak. The hike to Cerro Alto goes to the left here ascending sharply up a narrow trail.

My friends opted for the more leisurely walk to the left along the broad fireroad that eventually generates the trail that descends back to the campground through a wet woodland of trees and ferns. I decided to push on to the top.

Roads and firebreaks criss-cross the hills providing mountain bikes a labyrinthian system of trails that eventually run over to meet the TV Tower Road, or Cuesta Ridge Road. The road from the top of the Cuesta Grade formerly ran continuously along the Cuesta Ridge and down into the Morro Creek drainage until it met Route 41 at Cerro Alto Campground. Heavy rains years back washed out this road; Cerro Alto Peak can also be reached from the existing road on the top of Cuesta Ridge.

The trail to the top works the edge of a canyon, then runs across the narrowest part where bay trees grow and a stream trickles in wet weather. The trail gets steep and I felt sweat running down my back, even though the morning was cool. I saw a little poison oak along the way and some beautiful, blue hounds tongue (*Cynoglossum grande*).

At a curve of 1.4 miles, and 20 minutes after I left my group, the view of the ocean popped into view. This is a good stopping place if you don't want to go all the way; but in ten more minutes you can reach the top and have a window seat to the world.

The last ten minutes to the peak is a no-nonsense trudge that'll make the ticker clang. Close to the peak the trail comes out onto a roadway that winds around the peak to the left.

I had lunch with a few soaring hawks at this two-mile point. To the east I could see Atascadero and beyond to the Temblor Range. Below me to the southeast there is a placid little lake rimmed with tall trees. To the south Tassajara Peak Electronic Site appeared close by on the Cuesta Ridge Road, and beyond that I could see all the way to Point Sal. On the north the view stretched out to Piedras Blancas.

I hiked back down to where I left my friends and traced their footsteps along the AT&T cable road toward the ferny canyon.

After 20 minutes I came to a gully where the trail rises sharply on the other side. A small trail goes to the left. Through a grove of bay trees festooned with bearded lichens I entered the fern section where maidenhair, sword and wood ferns grow in abundance. The trail eventually comes down to a babbling creek, and follows it closely into the campground.

The total time to Cerro Alto and back via the ferny canyon is about four hours, or less than three hours if you turn left at the first trail junction along the level AT&T cable road.

Cerro Alto Campground is a National Forest facility providing drinking water, toilets and woodland campsites along the creek. Sites 1–8 are exceptionally pretty, next to small waterfalls and ripping brooks—favorites for picnicking. There is no fee for day use.

John Tembrock and Ann Colwell get docent Mary Coffeen's
informed interpretation along the trail to Cerro Alto.

The rock has an extensive tapestry of paintings in red, yellow and black.

23—Painted Rock—An Ancient Indian Site on the Perfect Back Road

It's exhilarating to find a perfect back road in the country where neither human nor habitation is seen and where the wild creatures lie in the roadway.

Before the time of Bureau of Land Management and Nature Conservancy stewardship, this was open range land where a drive often included cutting cattle, bumping calves and dividing a flock of sheep into two bleating halves.

This faraway place is the Carrisa Plains and California Valley, some 50 miles east of Santa Margarita on Route 58.

The road winds eastward out of Santa Margarita across burned hills and oak parklands until the trees thin and the grasses predominate.

After 15 miles we passed LaPanza Road and shortly came to Shell Creek Road (Commatti Road on some maps). An old Chicago Aeromotor windmill sits in a field of wildflowers along Shell Creek, across the road from the Avenales Wildlife Area (not to be confused with the city of Avenal 60 miles north).

One hundred yards from the intersection of Shell Creek Road a dirt lane goes off to the left through fields of wildflowers. We walked through this natural park of trees and meadows where splotches of baby blue eyes popped out of masses of yellow tidy tips and sunshine flowers (gold-fields). Robin and kildeer flitted through our view creating scenes as romantic as 19th century paintings of English gardens.

The Sinton family, of the Avenales Ranch, has graciously set aside a ten-mile section (north) along Shell Creek for wildflower viewing, and this area is probably one of the most colorful spring floral shows around.

103

The hills give way to plains and the valley of Carizzo (an Indian name for bunch grass), lay before us as flat as a Dakota prairie.

To the left we saw row upon row of glimmering-shimmering monstrosities. The devices snapped into new configurations of dazzling light as we drove eastward.

Arco Solar took a tip from the Indians and has assembled 800 trackers mounted on 40-foot columns that pivot and rotate photovoltaic panels and mirrors into the face of the sun. Operating on a 20-year computerized clock they simultaneously shift their 40-foot square plates into the sun every few minutes. We stood there entranced as they all groaned a few degrees to the west. [The Arco Solar Plant was sold in 1989.]

These photovoltaics produce about six megawatts of electricity, enough for about 3000 people.

From the Arco Solar Plant we turned off Route 58 onto Simmler-Soda Lake-San Diego Road, to the only service station-restaurant in California Valley. This is the center of a community that was promoted in 1960 to include schools, a shopping center, swimming pools, a golf course and 25,000 acres of 2½-acre plots for a community of 9000. In the 1960 hearings before the county supervisors, Fred Kimball wished developer Rick Walker success, "I hope you find oceans of water out there."

They didn't. Now only 200 people are scattered out on the grid of desolate streets that dead-end into the San Andreas Fault and the Temblor Range on the eastern side.

The road from the service station-restaurant curves past the fire house and the air strip where fields of fiddleneck undulate in the wind.

Six miles south of the service station we saw Soda Lake on the left, silvery white in the afternoon sun. At a little utility shack we turned onto a dirt road for a closer look and were surprised to see that most of the 3500 acre lake is nothing more than a bed of white crystalline soda (sodium carbonate). This lake teams with migratory arctic waterfowl in the winter, but most had already gone. Birdwatchers come during the winter rainy months to admire thousands of sandhill cranes who rest overnight in the shallow water of Soda Lake.

Near the end of Soda Lake, and 12 miles south of the gas station, we came to a little spur to the right. At the far end of that dirt road, I could see a horseshoe-shaped rock which resembled my mental picture of the famous Indian Painted Rock.

Four miles away, through fields of wheat and over green hills, the ranch road approaches the rock.

Painted Rock is a historic landmark and archaeological site of ancient Indian art, located in an isolated section of the county adjacent to thousands of acres of Bureau of Land Management holdings in the Caliente Mountains.

It has recently been designated the Carrizo Plain Natural Area, a 180,000-acre preserve of ranchlands and BLM wilderness that has been cooperatively acquired by The Nature Conservancy, the California Department of Fish and Game, and the BLM. The area will be managed as a wildlife habitat and recreation area.

A campground is scheduled for development on Soda Lake Road, ten miles south of the old ranch road to Painted Rock, and a visitors' center and lookout point will be located just west of Soda Lake, at the north end of the natural area.

Painted Rock is an impressive cone-shaped mass of gray sandstone, 200 feet high, 1000 feet across, with a 20-foot portal into a circular amphitheatre measuring 200 x 120 feet. The interior walls converge toward the top, giving the ground level walls protection from the elements.

The shamans, Chumash mystics and diviners of the origin of man, painted mythological characters and figures on the flat walls. There is Coyote and Lizard and many variations of the Sun. The left side of the cave has an extensive tapestry of paintings in red, yellow and black, but a lot of it has been chipped away by souvenir hunters, shot by vandals or eroded by weather.

At the turn of the century, ranchers used the enclosure for housing sheep, penning as many as 4000 overnight.

While I pondered the mystery of these ancient rock paintings, my friend scrambled up the outside of the rock and perched on top, 200 feet above me, a miniscule figure on this gargantuan rock temple.

"I came, I saw, I conquered!" she screamed.

"Big deal," I thought. "Anybody can do that. Now let's see, how did she get up there? OK, here's a toe hold... and then I can walk on four points to there . . ."

I discovered that 5000 years of Indian scramblings over that rock have created a pathway of steps and ascents to the top. Eventually we sat together looking out on a scene that through the ages "abounded in wild horses, elk, deer and antelope in countless numbers, and myriads of migratory birds of the arctic in their season, feeding upon its herbage." (Myron Angel) No wonder the Indians stayed so long.

If *you're* looking for that perfect back road where neither human nor habitation is seen, take Soda Lake Road to Route 166, then west to Santa Maria and Route 101 back home. Total mileage to SLO is 232 via this circuit, versus 150 miles if you return via Route 58.

San Antonio Mission (1771) was the third California mission.

24—Through Almond Orchards to the Old Hearst Ranch Headquarters and San Antonio Mission

If you follow El Camino north, it runs right through Jolon, the commercial and social center of the San Antonio Valley—or so I had been told.

In search of this megalopolis, we got off Route 101 on 24th Street (Route 46 exit) in Paso Robles and turned left through town. This becomes G14, or Nacimiento Lake Drive, a wonderfully scenic road traversing the gentle hills ablush in spring with flowering almonds.

The trees undulate up and over the knolls like stripes on a flag. For miles and miles manicured orchards sing the joyous message of spring. "For whatsoever a man sows, that shall he also reap," is the lesson of the hills. Years of good husbandry have produced a scene as blessed and full as any idealized image of America.

G14 leaves the almond orchards ten miles north of Paso Robles, running through hills of blue and valley oak to the Nacimiento Reservoir dam. After a few miles G14 becomes Interlake Road and slides between Nacimiento Reservoir on the left and San Antonio Reservoir on the right. Eventually we came to a large open plain and the town of Lockwood. G14 turns left onto Jolon Road at the Lockwood store and continues along to the town of Jolon.

Other than a mom and pop motorcycle gang at the Ruby Mine Saloon (circa 1948), there wasn't anything doing; nothing that looked like a commercial and social center that reportedly served the San Antonio Valley at the turn of the century. Even the waitress in the saloon didn't know there was anything else, except "some old buildings down G14, about a quarter of a mile, that have been there for a long time."

That woman has a knack for understatement. Sure enough, there it was. The Jolon of yesteryear that functioned from 1848-1948. All that's left of the adobe Dutton Hotel is a few walls that hardly hold window frames. The old Episcopal church is in good repair and still being used, but across El Camino the old Tidball store-hotel-post office-residence-lunch counter and saloon (circa 1878) hangs on following a fire in 1972. It was retired in 1948 when Ramona Sutfin, the last owner, moved over to Mission Road with her new Ruby Mine Saloon.

That's it for a town that flourished in 1880, supplying ranchers and miners, and boasting a valley population of about 700 people, and a town of two hotels, three stores, one saloon, a blacksmith shop and eight residences. In 1886 the railroad reached King City and the highway moved east to intersect with the railroad. El Camino was no longer the main route and Jolon began to fade.

We went back to the Ruby Mine Saloon where we picked up the Mission Road to Hunter Liggett Military Reservation and the San Antonio Mission. Hunter Liggett is a field maneuver and training area that plays host to armored units from bases around the country. Units bring in their own tanks through Camp Roberts, which is tied to Hunter Liggett by a tank trail.

Down Mission Road we passed a helicopter field and a depot of tanks and armored vehicles. On the right we saw an imposing Spanish-style building with a gold dome. It didn't look military to me so I began snooping around. The scoop is that this was the William Randolph Hearst ranch headquarters, built in 1931 and designed by Julia Morgan, the architect of Hearst Castle.

It's constructed on the grounds of the old Milpitas Ranch House, an adobe-frame structure that Hearst first used as the center of his 149,000 acre ranch where he managed 50,000 head of cattle. Hearst called it his "Hacienda Milpitas Ranch House." It contained a comfortable three-bedroom house for the manager, rooms for the ranch hands, a number of beautifully-appointed guest rooms, a "bull room" where the cowboys entertained, a dining room and kitchen facilities. It was fully landscaped with mature plantings of trees and shrubs.

The army uses the building now and is presently restoring it. Because the building is on the National Register of Historic Buildings, all repairs are done according to the original 1931 specifications. Although the building is not open to the public, a walk around it is very worthwhile.

Hearst sold part of his ranch in 1941, and with the sale went the hacienda and town of Jolon. Presently, Hunter Liggett owns all the land north of the Nacimiento River and everything west to the coastal range ridge, an area of about 185,000 acres. More than 15,000 troops can train here at one time.

Off in a low lying plain at the end of Mission Road, we saw the 1771 San Antonio Mission, considerably more modest and inconspicuous than Hearst's village on the hill.

This mission was the third of 21 built from 1769–1823. Much of it had fallen into desperate conditions but Hearst generously gave funds to restore the mission to its present state. The chapel is the only building that did not collapse and is the highlight of the mission. Extensive archaeological diggings by Dr. Robert Hoover of Cal Poly University are reconstructing the history of this mission. You may want to join in the discoveries by signing up for a summer course of field work here.

We had gone to find Jolon. It hardly exists, but the ride to obscurity is along a path of flowers, lakes and historic masterpieces.

To get home fast take Jolon Road to Route 101, then zip home south. The round trip from San Luis Obispo is about 130 miles.

Here are a few loops that are good for viewing the flowering almonds in the vicinity of Atascadero and Paso Robles. Out of Atascadero take Route 41 east and turn left on Templeton Road, right on South El Pomar Drive to Almond Drive. Turn left through almond orchards to El Pomar Drive, then left to Templeton Road, right to Vineyard Drive back to Route 101.

On the south end of Paso Robles, take 6th Street west to Peachy Canyon Road out into the country, left to Willow Creek, left on Oakdale over to Route 46.

The 1931 Hearst Ranch house is headquarters for Fort Hunter Liggett.

Nacimiento-Ferguson Road skirts the ridges high above Route 1.

25—Nacimiento-Ferguson Road—
It Used to be a Burro Trail

One of my favorite country back roads is Nacimiento-Ferguson Road. I inevitably end up on this trans-coastal route when I want to show friends and out-of-town guests the best face of the Central Coast.

On the east side is the historic Jolon Valley, with the San Antonio Mission and the 1930s Hearst ranch headquarters building, and on the west side is Route 1 and the infinite Pacific Ocean stretching to the ends of our imagination.

Between the coast and Jolon is a beautifully-paved road that parallels the headwaters of Nacimiento River on the east and Mill Creek on the west side. Near the top of the ridge the road winds tightly in and out of the canyons where redwoods and cypress grow along creeks cast in dim blue light.

Pherbe Luchessa recalls traveling over the old trail that predates this road. She would accompany her father as they went into Jolon for provisions (around 1912).

"How was it, going over that trail in those early years, Pherb?" I asked.

"Very tiresome. It was an all day thing. And very slow. But...we did it a lot of times. Usually I ended up on an old burro—an old gray burro. There were no wagons—just old burros. The trail was only this wide," she said, illustrating with her little arms outstretched.

Ramona (Duck) Sutfin, who used to own the Tidball store in Jolon, remembers the WPA men working on the trail in the '30s, raising it from trail status to a dirt road. Even in the '60s and '70s it wasn't anything to brag about; but, today, your car or motorhome will be on very good blacktop up one side and down the other.

It's about 70 miles from San Luis Obispo to the San Antonio Mission, at the end of G18 (east of King City). At the Ruby Mine Saloon we turned left on Mission Road and passed through the guarded gate to Fort Hunter Liggett. The MP told us we could get through to the coast but that we may have a wait because maneuvers were taking place.

A few miles past the gate we turned left on Nacimiento-Ferguson Road where a small stone cairn and memorial plaque are erected in memory of Lieutenant Robert Ferguson who gave his life in Viet Nam. He was the son of General Ferguson, commander of Fort Ord.

We crossed over Stony Creek on a bridge while scurrying military vehicles splashed through the river on the old road below. The road then courses through a parkland of oak trees strung with lichens (Spanish moss). The wildflowers in this area have been wildly colorful, rivaling the Avenales Wildlife Area east of Santa Margarita on Route 58, but get there by May for a really good show.

A few miles further we came to a roadstop where an MP popped out of a small shed to inform us there was warfare ahead, and we would have to wait 45 minutes for the war to end. It was noon, so we pulled into the shade of the trees and opened the cooler for a trunk lunch. Troop carriers, jeeps and strange looking vehicles hurried up and down the road like insects. Soon the laser war was over and we were back on the road.

About 14 miles past the gate we entered the Los Padres National Forest and left behind the rutted tank trail scenery of Hunter Liggett. Nacimiento River gurgles along the left side of the road and alders grow in lush stands along the shores. There are numerous places to stop and several rustic campgrounds are ideal for picnics or overnight stays.

We passed Ponderosa Campground at 16.5 miles from the gate and came to Nacimiento Campground at 19.2 miles. The trees were getting taller and greener as the turns in the road tightened. Soon we spotted blooming dogwoods and caught the sight of redwoods up a canyon.

At 23 miles from the gate we crested the ridge and drove past the U.S. Forest Service Fire Station. The Central Coast Ridge Road cuts across Nacimiento-Ferguson Road, going north to Vincente Trail (four miles), San Antonio Trail (four miles), and Cone Peak Trail (six miles). The Forest Service at King City has details on these trails and back country campsites. Call (408) 385-5434 for information.

To the left, or south, the South Ridge Road traverses the ridge for awhile then dips down to Route 1, becoming Plaskett Ridge Road near Jade Beach (a mile north of Gorda).

As we drove the west side of Nacimiento-Ferguson Road along the Mill Creek drainage, we caught fleeting views of the ocean, then came to a pullout on the left where we all piled out to walk a descending grassy terrace. The scene from here is of a steep, lush canyon where water runs and redwoods grow. This canyon was logged at the turn of the century but is looking pristine and natural again.

Out toward the sea we saw the road curving along the outside edges of the consecutive ridges that descend towards Route 1. The ocean was a transparent turquoise mass, with gobs of dark green kelp suspended, falling and rising with the sea like a huge bowl of jello.

As we descended on the road to Route 1 and the mouth of Mill Creek, we passed through stands of laurel and maples, and more redwoods along the creeks. On Route 1 we turned left to the entrance to Mill Creek Beach. Winter storms bring new samples of jade to the beach, and millions of perfectly rounded pebbles shine from the pounding surf, waiting to be examined and caressed.

It's just more perfection after a ride through country that has to be seen to be appreciated. The loop trip from San Luis Obispo and back takes about six hours, not counting the wars, and is 225 miles.

From the top we saw a lush green valley running to the sea.

The limekilns were used for making cement in the 1880s.

26—Limekilns, Jade Coves and Redwoods in Far Away Places Close By

I will go down to the lovely Sur Rivers and dip my
arms in them up to the shoulders. I will find my ac-
counting where the Alder leaf quivers and the ocean
wind over the river boulders. . . where I will find
things and things, and no more thoughts.

Robinson Jeffers

As we stared into the inferno of our campfire at the Limekiln Campground,
I marveled that living so simply in the outdoors can be so enjoyable—
and wondered why we have become so complex.

The flickering images of the fire conjured up memories . . . of family
dogs and childhood days, and the paths of our lives that brought us to this
place. The fog of day gave way to a clear night and stars shone and a sky
of infinite darkness laid us to rest.

No better place to do this than in the Santa Lucia Mountains, and
a place of great intrigue is the Limekiln Beach Redwood Campground
12 miles from Gorda, an hour and a half drive up Route 1 from San Luis
Obispo.

The ocean surf is in one ear and the Limekiln Creek is in the other.
A visual panorama of redwoods and beach makes this camping spot the
delight of many who reserve favorite sites a year in advance. There are
beach sites, cliff sites and stream-side spots deep in the blue light of the
redwoods.

The limekilns date back to 1880 when the Rockland Cement Company fired the limestone in four huge metal kilns that were brought in by
schooners from England. At the mouth of the canyon ships arrived to
carry out the timber and the limestone to San Francisco, and to bring

supplies to the local residents who carted their goods over narrow mountain roads to homes in the hills.

It has been one hundred years since those early settlers logged the big trees and burned the slash in the kilns, but the canyons have had time to heal, and cathedral rings of redwoods have grown up around the old stumps. The water is clear and every inch of the forest floor is crowded with sorrel and ferns.

The half-mile trail to the falls is strewn with fallen logs lying helter skelter across the creek. The water cascades down 120 feet, crashing against the boulders, spraying everything an emerald green.

Photographers have a tough time hiking the half-mile trail to the kilns and falls. Every turn produces another vision of such idyllic woodland imagery that they spin and shoot in wild ecstasy. (Light levels are extremely low, so take a tripod.)

Six hundred sixty acres of this privately-owned campground are surrounded by thousands of acres of wilderness of the Los Padres National Forest. Steelhead trout, planted here in 1890 from fish captured in the Big Sur River, can be caught in the streams right in the campground. There is surf fishing and sunning at the privately-owned beach.

The campground is well organized and bright flowers smile from the roadsides. Hot showers and running water make the stay here comfortable. The waterfalls and limekilns are accessible only through the Limekiln Campground.

For those of you who find dew on your sleeping bag and smoke in your eyes less than paradise, there is a good civilized alternative.

When Highway 1 was completed in 1937, a little roadside lodge was constructed two miles north of Limekiln, on a narrow ledge between the road and the pounding surf. Lucia Lodge was built near the site of Lucia Dani's post office and trailside restaurant. Lucia's brothers carried the mail by horseback over the Santa Lucia Mountains from King City when the limekilm was closed in 1885 and Lucia became the post mistress. When the highway opened, the post office moved 20 miles north to Big Sur; but the place still bears Lucia's name.

Wilbur Harlan homesteaded these parts in 1895 and had ten children, guaranteeing that Lucia Lodge and all the land around would be the empire of Harlans. Ken and Keith Harlan run the lodge and restaurant today and sell gasoline and basic food supplies to travelers.

The 50-year-old cabins, with open-beamed ceilings and piney furniture, are set 500 feet above Lucia Bay. Rock gardens and flowers adorn the grounds and on Harlan Point you can sit imagining times when Wilbur Harlan would hire a ship to bring supplies into the harbor, and the family mule would strain to haul them up to the cliff top.

Breakfast in the morning on the sunny deck overlooking the ocean is an especially pleasant experience. An attractive assortment of breakfast items is served.

On the way home I made some unusual discoveries.

Five miles south of the Limekiln Campground is Pacific Valley Center, offering groceries or lunch. Their homemade breads and pies are a bit of the old-fashioned goodness you still find along this rural highway.

Going south from Pacific Valley Center there are a number of stiles (staircases over a fence) going out on to the terraces. Don't mind the grazing cattle, it's all U.S. Forest Service land, open to the public. The walks to the cliff ledges are like the first sights of exotic lands. Lonely white sand beaches and gray-green sculptured headlands awash in foaming white water are hidden from roadside views.

An extraordinary walk is at Sand Dollar Beach, about a mile or two south of Pacific Valley. Here, and at Jade Cove and Willow Creek, jade hunters lie on their bellies scooping through tons of beautiful pebbles hiding nuggets of jade. It's almost a sure bet you'll find some good specimens.

At the town of Gorda, the Big Sur Jade Company welcomes your visit. They're up a staircase above the store among a melange of benches, motors, grinding wheels and sanders that transform field pieces into table tops, bookends and jewelry.

Electric service hasn't reached beyond San Simeon, and rural simplicity and natural order are the refreshing rewards for those who linger awhile on our northern coast.

For information call or write:

Limekiln Beach Redwood Campground
Big Sur 93920 (408) 667-2403

Lucia Lodge
Highway 1, Big Sur 93920 (408) 667-2391

Sprays of light break the darkness along the cave trail.

27—Pinnacles National Monument— Hiking in Caves, Cliffs and Streams

I know for some of you hiking is associated with pain, sweat, drudgery and long hours in the sun. But I've got good news. Hiking at Pinnacles National Monument is exciting, daring and a lot of whoopee in underground caverns, stumbling over boulders, tripping through creeks and squeezing between crevices so narrow your feet get stuck.

We began our hike on the east side of Pinnacles and decided a good day hike would be from Bear Gulch Visitor Center along the Moses Spring Trail (.7 mile) to the reservoir. The trail begins innocently enough, through a setting of digger pine and blue oak, but soon gets barmy.

In a steep canyon a great mass of volcanic boulders has rolled in, sealing off the sunlight. We came to the first cave which was not much more than a long hallway; then, in another 200-yards, a set of caves through which a small stream meandered. Water-sculpted caverns of volcanic rock formed fascinating grottoes of the walls and ceilings. Sprays of light from above broke the darkness, giving the walkway an eerie atmosphere.

As the darkness deepened, we floundered into an underground world of tipping rock and rounded boulders. The air became biting cold and I wished for a warmer sweater. Ahead of us water cascaded down a smooth slide, splashed again the floor and babbled past us.

From the stream bed a staircase of cement stairs, with a stout metal handrail, rose steeply to a balcony lookout where we saw more cascading water percolating through the rock.

At one point we jumped off the balcony onto a gravel trail that led to a large circular room where water ran down the walls. It reminded me of the Madonna Inn men's room.

Higher and higher we climbed. Sometimes the staircases were tiny and spiraling, but then would discontinue, and there would be nothing more than a few ascending stepping stones. We crouched and squirmed through narrow clefts that would make a fat man sweat. My friend insisted I was crazy for pushing on, but occasionally a friendly arrow on the wall assured me we were on the right track.

Now the path led directly into the middle of the stream. A few stepping stones kept us mostly out of the water as we inched forward.

"I don't know which way to go from here. What do you think?" my friend called.

"You tell me, you've got the light."

The light searched the walls and the floor, and for a long moment we thought and looked and thought and looked. There was a small opening to the left. My friend led on, grudgingly sharing the light while I took my turn at grumbling about someone taking me up a creek without a . . . turn around. Next time I'll bring my very own light. I accused her of getting us "good and lost."

"No, we are not lost!" she shrilled from up front where she was splashing, groping like a drunk along the cave walls. I clumsily tripped along in the murky behind, *pleading* for a few beams to lighten my way. Not only were we in water, we were in a half crouch, bumping our heads and scraping our packs on the roof and walls.

Thousands of spelunkers, I'm sure, have followed this same trail, going from despair to pure joy and laughter with the discovery and adventure of crawling through 23-million-year-old volcanic rock, laced with trickling waterways.

Tree roots appeared along the ceilings and walls like snakes. The digger pines up on the surface have been known to plumb 150 feet for water. I tickled them as I went by to let them know we were down here in their water.

We were lost again. The path petered out and led us into a solid rock. We backed up a few paces and examined the walls. A small unexpected opening to the right led to another obscure opening, and another, and finally into a large room flooded with yellow light that was ricocheting off the boulders above. A steep staircase of chipped steps led to the full sunlight, past an iron gate. The gate is closed to down traffic during storms and flash floods and bears a warning.

We stood in the sunshine and enjoyed the warmth and smells of a living world while recapping this exhilirating experience. If you have kids, you must take them for a hike through this magic mountain. They'll love it!

There is a trail that returns to the Bear Gulch Visitor Center via a .7 mile loop, but we opted for the hike along the reservoir up to Scout Peak at 2651 feet. This is a steady two-mile uphill trek that gets the body ready for lunch at the top.

There's a saddle along the ridge up at Scout Peak with a bench where we sat and contemplated the pinnacles and the soggy sandwiches at the bottom of our pack.

The story about this mountain is that 20-million years ago, down by Lancaster, 190 miles south, a series of volcanos poured out 8000 feet of molten rhyolite. After the cooling and settling of the land, two north-south trending faults were formed through this volcanic zone. The Pacific Plate moved half of the volcanic pinnacles north an inch a year until they reached King City. The remaining volcanic pinnacles are 190 miles south at Lancaster, on the North American Plate.

During the faulting, cracks and fissures produced deep canyons. Erosion of the joints eventually created the vertical columns and spires that give Pinnacles its name. Over a mile of the volcanic rhyolite has eroded away, the highest peak now being only 3303 feet.

We took the High Peaks Trail through these megaliths and spires using the hacked toe holds and handrails; sometimes going across the face of great boulders, sometimes walking sideways through narrow cracks. It's another experience of such diversity and adventure I'm sure the same CCC gang that had fun in the caves was up here chortling as they made zigzagging trails through the Pinnacles.

We met Tony Steever, from St. Louis, Missouri; Bill and Eileen Cox, from Effingham, Illinois; and a couple of guys from the bay area that come here for technical rock climbing. We didn't meet anybody from San Luis Obispo.

The trail down the Condor Gulch Trail brought us back to the Bear Gulch Visitor Center, a total round trip of 6.5 miles, enough for one day considering we gained about 1400 feet going up.

The east side of Pinnacles, and the beginning of the caves walk along the Moses Spring Trail, is reached via G13 from Route 101 at King

The east side of Pinnacles, and the beginning of the caves walk along the Moses Spring Trail, is reached via G13 from Route 101 at King City. It's a 35-mile road traversing soft, green mountainous hills and giant valleys, with old ranch houses wrapped in summer porches. This good two-lane road ties into Route 25 and then Route 146 into the park.

Just before entering the Monument there is Pinnacles Campground, a private facility with all the amenities, including a pool ((408) 389-4462). It's a beautiful campground in a riparian setting, only a short walk to the trails of the park. If you're driving a motorhome or hauling a trailer, this is the side to come to. The distance from San Luis Obispo is about 113 miles.

The west side of the park can be reached from 101 at Soledad, along Route 146. Route 146 is 11 miles of banked sweeps, great for sport driving but big trouble for motorhomes and vehicles with trailers.

Camping on the west side is primitive. There are chemical toilets and running water only, no hookups, no services. But day hiking is very good from the west side. I particularly like the Balcony Trail hike that goes 1.1 miles through the caves, then up over the top of the caves past the Balcony Cliffs and Machette Ridge. This pleasant round trip hike of three miles is varied and picturesque. Numerous lookout points can make lunching and sunning a full afternoon activity.

The next time you're looking for an outdoor experience with a lot of laughs bundle up the kids and take a ride to Pinnacles National Monument—and don't forget to bring flashlights.

A hiker observes Machette Ridge on the Balcony Cliffs trail.

Index